ANI… FIZ…

TRIP… F…

C000176901

Associate Chef Terry Pritchard

Creative Consultant Mike Margolis
Photography Gered Mankowitz

CHAMELEON

'Welcome to my World
Give yourself a break
Get yourself uncurled
Change your body shape
I promise you will find
With every breath you take
Direction in your mind
With every move you make

It's the Fizz. It's the bubble. It's the biz.
It's the fizz. It's the sparkle, yes it is.
It's the shape, it's the smile, it's the joy,
it's the style!
It's the fizz, Yes it is, it's the fizz!

It's the path. It's the road. It's a ride!
It's a blast. It'll last. It's a glide!
It is work, it is play and it's fun either way,
It's the fizz, yes it is, it's the fizz!'

From the opening number of the ANITA HARRIS FIZZICAL
video 'The Fizz' by Margolis/Clayton

First published in Great Britain in 1998 by Chameleon Books,
an imprint of André Deutsch Ltd,
76 Dean Street, London W1V 5HA
André Deutsch is a VCI plc company

Copyright © CPEAL
All rights reserved

ISBN 0 233 99358 4

Food Stylist: Sunil
Additional photo coverage: Hugh Turvey at Mankowitz Studios
Book design: Linda Wade
Fizzical music published by CPEAL

CONTENTS

THE PROGRAMME

CURTAIN UP

ACT ONE

ACT TWO

ACT THREE

THE PLAYERS

Thanks to: TERRY PRITCHARD, my ebullient Australian associate chef and culinary capers companion, whose way with a wok, palaver with a pannikin, cheek with chicken, sashay with a saucepan and camp with a colander, has been a lesson to us all. Terry is a Columbus of the kitchen, New World, new ways. An adventurous swashbuckler of sauté, soufflé and savouries, Terry is The Fizz from Oz (with added zappy frappé!). GERED MANKOWITZ for, as always, photography you could eat. Gered and I go back to well . . . we go back. His glorious colour photographs have decorated my theatre posters and now deliciously depict my menus and illustrate this book. My cous-cous runneth over. Gered has the Photographic Fizz. KENNY CLAYTON, who has gifted this project with mouth-watering music and witty lyrics with a flavour to savour. Kenny is a cross between Paderewski and Anton Mossiman: he cooks like Paderewski and plays the piano like Anton! Jesting aside (and slightly to the right) Kenny is a constant inspiration. He is an acknowledged spaghetti supremo, a master of wine (well, he's a musician, what would you expect?) and unquestionably has the Philharmonic Fizz. LOUISE DIXON, managing editor of my publisher André Deutsch, her smile and enthusiasm light up every meeting. VCI's PAUL HEMBURY and CAROLE GASKILL, executive producers of the Fizzical Video, who joined the Fizz.

STEVE AYRES, CEO of VCI for the phone call. JUDY TARLO, publicist and friend, whose beautifully prepared Sunday brunches have made Jude a legend for her own lunch time. Aerobics champion coach PETER STEPHENS and his assistant NORMAN PERRY, who did the business with fizzness. BENNY BALL, magician and master of light whose exquisite work can be seen on the companion video. IRVING DAVIES who choreographed the Fizz dance sequences on the Fizzical video, my buddy and constant mentor. Irv' has the everlasting, effervescent Fizz (and frankly, I new knew him when he effer vosn't!). MIKE, my husband, for scripting, producing and directing the video, as record producer of my Fizzical CD, and for encouragement, exhilarating arguments and ideas. Mike is also a wily wok wizard and is my Wiz behind the Fizz. Thanks for many tips from my brother DAVID, a significant chef who, before he became a corporate magnate, trained in cuisine at Écolè Hotelière de Lausanne, and brother PHILIP who courageously tested many of the recipes. Phil is in aviation and can pilot his way into any kitchen where something good is on the hob. My parents ERIC and MARION, who began the Fizz and continued to practise it and gift it to others throughout their lives. My mother was a phenomenal cook and much of her is within these pages.

PROLOGUE
It's Showtime!

RIGHT! You've picked up this book because you're looking for a change in yourself (or for someone else to change?). Maybe knock off a few pounds? Shape-up? Cholesterol conscious? Whatever, you're giving it all some thought, right now.

GOOD! Let's get Fizzical!

We all have to deal with the day.Get up, get out there, get on with it, go to the office, get the kids off to school, get the shopping. In my case, get my body on that stage and 'give it the old razzle dazzle'.What can help?

This is a book about preparing, cooking and serving food for health and to feel good within yourself and about yourself.This is a book about physical fitness. You are what you eat, it affects how you look and feel...

YOU CAN REMODEL YOURSELF BY THE WAY YOU MOVE AND HOW YOU EAT

It is not Mission Impossible. I am not a naturally slim person. From an early age I wrestled with weight and shape problems and my life has been a constant contest with the bulgy bits. If I'm not careful, my lower half can expand like a melted candle, everything gathering together for a meeting at the bottom! So...

BUMS AND THIGHS OVERSIZE? DON'T DRAMATISE – EXERCISE!

When I was thirteen I was knocked over on the ice rink and damaged the base of my spine. I discovered that when I exercised the pain disappeared and that it returned when I didn't. So, I did and I do. The need to keep the base of my spine flexible has influenced my fitness programme. Over the years my own personal exercise system has evolved from many disciplines – dance, yoga, aerobics, martial arts movements and good old-fashioned 'keep moving – keep fit!'I call my regime the Triple F System, the three Fs signifying regimes for Fitness, Food and Feelgood.

I don't believe in Thin. Slim and Trim are something quite different. I am not a fan of the word 'diet' – a word associated with 'fasting' and having a really nasty time. This book is about the enjoyment that goes with eating properly, the dynamic effect it has on your entire lifestyle, and the fun that can be had in the kitchen creating great-tasting nourishment. Fizzical Food is fun!

If you really need to lose pounds in a rush, you'll find the Fatburner section really works and gives you an energy charge you won't believe until you've tried it. (Then you won't stop talking about it!)

There is a companion Fizzical! video to this book, and a CD which features songs specially composed for the video. All the lyrics have a message or amusing and inspiring comments to make about the business of staying in shape. Some of these lyrics decorate this book as memory jogs and mottoes of encouragement. Catch phrases help to keep you in line. One I have carried with me all my life (and now it's set to music I can sing it too) is to tell myself:

'EVERY DAY, AND IN EVERY WAY
I FEEL BETTER AND BETTER
AND BETTER'

Not sure about that? Try it. Give yourself a regular eyeball-to-eyeball kick up the umm-che-rah-rah!

Fizzical Food collects together a selection of my favourite recipes, with some new twists encompassing a whole range of good-for-you, great-to-look-at and utterly delicious drinks, snacks, breakfasts, barbecues, main courses, à-la-carte menus and desserts. Food to enhance mind, body and spirit.

There is no need for you to make radical changes to your normal eating habits – in fact, they should improve. To cope with my lifestyle I have had to fashion food to fit the moment. So, for example, you too might find Food on the Move a useful chapter. Designed to help you ease-on-down during those busy days in the office or when you're charging around at home, when food isn't a priority but you know you'll feel that much better if you eat healthily, as well as heartily, and with a minimum of fuss.

SOMETIMES IT TAKES A SHOCK TO THE SYSTEM TO GALVANISE US INTO REPAIR MODE

We all know that one of the biggest health hazards in the western world is heart disease. There is a fast-growing awareness of its causes and how to avoid them. Most heart attacks happen as a result of stress or because of what we put into our mouths. Mike, my husband, made a wonderful cardiac recovery but surgery was needed, and we both realised and understood the truth of another antique saying:

PREVENTION IS BETTER THAN CURE

This book is inspired by that golden rule.

Why do so many of us wait for a health scare or some other dramatic shock signal to wake us up to getting our act together? You actually know when you need to get sorted. What you do (or don't do) about it affects others as well as yourself. You need to share how you feel with your partner, it's fair to you and yours and it helps. Sharing fitness can be fun, and all it takes is:

A MINIMUM WORKOUT –
TWENTY MINUTES A DAY.
THE WARM-UP AND JUST ONE OTHER PROGRAMME FROM THE FIZZICAL VIDEO WILL GIVE YOU THAT MINIMUM WORKOUT.

High blood pressure and too much of the wrong cholesterol can be controlled by what we eat. We can add two more Fs to my three Fs – *Fibre* and *Fish*. We now know that fibre is a vitally important part of our food intake – fruit, vegetables, grains and pulses – and we all need more than is generally realised, so Fizzical Food provides some new ways to palatably partake. Fish is wonderful for the heart, particularly fish with a high-oil content. People from nations which favour food from the deep have a low incidence of cardiac disease. Find me an Eskimo who has a problem of the heart and I'll bet it's romantic, not Icelandic.

We're going to favour fibre and fish and say a fond farewell to some formidable fats, and, FIZZ NEWS-FLASH! ''the message is getting through! Awareness is on the increase; heart disease is on the retreat. Stay away from demon saturated fats, cook with olive oil and consume plenty of fish oil. The good news is that having read this far, you've just joined a group that is becoming tuned-in''.

Life is made up of goals and achievements. Stick-to-it-ness is important. Stay with me and learn how to improve your lifestyle, be adventurous in the kitchen, wholesome in your eating habits and enjoy an exhilarating world of fitness, feelgood and fun. Feeling good makes you look good.

IT'S THE FIZZ!
IT'S THE BUBBLE!
IT'S THE BIZ!

Let's go!
Let's go!
Let's go!

CURTAIN UP
FIZZICAL EATING
7 POINT BLUEPRINT FOR LONG LIFE

Nowadays there is a whole casserole of confusion about what is good and what's bad for us. Most people's first impulse is to ignore the lot and 'let nature take its course'. However, taking a large kitchen knife to the facts and figures, cutting away the fat as it were, leaves 7 essential elements I think you need to know (you will find some of this information repeated throughout the book to reinforce its importance).

1. Cholesterol

Some call it the nutritional nightmare. It is a fact that there is good and bad cholesterol; the stuff you need and the stuff you need to avoid or, better still, prevent. Enough cholesterol is produced naturally in our bodies so we don't actually need any more of it from food. A HIGH FAT DIET INCREASES THE CHOLESTEROL LEVEL IN THE BLOOD AND CAN LEAD TO HEART ATTACKS.

2. Fibre

Western diets are renowned for their lack of high dietary fibre. Fibre supplies the roughage which is essential for the normal operation of our digestive systems, encouraging food residues to be eliminated regularly from the body. Fibre is very low in fat and is found in grains, beans, pulses, root vegetables, brown rice, fresh and dried fruits and wholemeal breads. YOU CANNOT DO WITHOUT FIBRE.

3. Fish

Certain fish and other seafood contain oils that are immensely beneficial to good health. Among these are mackerel, herring, pilchards, sardines, tuna, salmon, anchovies, mullet, trout and oysters. It's no coincidence that cod liver oil is still taken to ease arthritis and rheumatism. FISH IS FAB!

4. Red Wine

A French proverb says, 'A glass of Beaujolais a day keeps the doctor away' (in French, of course!) My husband considers our doctor a first class fellow, mainly because he prescribed Mike a glass of claret every night. Red wine, in moderation, actually contributes to the prevention of heart disease.

5. Oils

Mono-unsaturated oils include olive and groundnut oil. Poly-unsaturated oils include those made from plant seeds, such as safflower, sunflower, sesame, corn and soyabean. ALL ARE GOOD FOR YOU.

6. Fat

Low fat, not no fat. You have to find the balance. Every body needs a certain amount of fat intake. Saturated fats, if eaten to excess, can increase levels of cholesterol in the blood. So, **AVOID BUTTER, CREAM, WHOLE MILK, MOST HARD AND HIGH-FAT SOFT CHEESES, AND MEAT FAT**. It can be a bit of a minefield wading through the new fat phraseology. WHEN YOU BUY, READ THE LABELS. Here's your quick check, easy-peasy:

FIZZ-FAT GUIDE

BAD

SATURATED FATS. Can raise blood cholesterol and can be factors in many illnesses. THESE ARE FATS TO AVOID.

Saturated fats are present in animal foods – **BUTTER, CREAM, MEAT FAT, CHEESE, POULTRY SKIN, LARD AND DRIPPING.**

GOOD

MONO–UNSATURATED FATS. Used to be thought of as having little effect one way or the other on cholesterol. Nowadays they are used extensively in eating programmes for a healthy heart.

Mono-unsaturated fats are present in **OLIVE OIL, OLIVES, PEANUTS, AVOCADOS**. Varying amounts are found in **VEGETABLE OILS, FISH AND POULTRY**.

GOOD

POLY-UNSATURATED FATS. These lessen the fat build-up on the walls of the arteries and reduce the wrong type of cholesterol in our blood. THE BLOCKING OF ARTERIES IS A MAJOR CAUSE OF HEART DISEASE.

Poly-unsaturated fats are present in **SOYA BEAN, SESAME AND GRAPE SEED, GRAINS, OILY FISH (SARDINES, HERRING, SALMON, TUNA, MACKEREL).**

7. Water

I try not to drink less than 1.5 litres (2 pints) a day to help clear out damaging toxins and cleanse the system. There is a respected body of opinion which recommends that, at meal times, water should be drunk before or after the meal, rather than during it. WATER IS A WISE INVESTMENT.

RECIPE NOTES

The number of 'servings per person' is denoted at the beginning of each Act's actual recipe section or, occasionally when necessary, just before a particular recipe itself.

All spoon measurements are flat unless otherwise indicated.

As an alternative to sugar, I suggest honey or sweeteners.

Salt. Let's not get paranoid about it. Most of us can cope very well with the 10 g (½ oz) we consume daily. However, people with high blood pressure and certain diseases of the heart, liver and kidney should take medical advice regarding their salt intake. Salt is, in fact, vital in our eating programme although we actually need just 1 g a day – we consume the other 9 g because we've grown to like it. Soy and Worcestershire sauce are good substitutes; whilst they contain salt, it is less concentrated. Sea salt is recommended.

Ice. Certain drinks in 'Act One: Kick Off with a Cocktail' contain crushed ice, but ice is not recommended in every cold drink. Providing liquids are chilled before use and consumed immediately, ice should remain an option.

Grilling, boiling, steaming and stir-frying are the best and most wholesome ways of cooking meat, fish and vegetables. If you have to roast (see my caution regarding saturated fats in Curtain Up, page 15), don't sit meat in dripping. Merely brush a little oil (see Essentials, page 20) over the meat. Remember, meat makes its own juices anyway. When you cook fish, wrapping it in foil will capture both the juice and its full flavour. And when you boil poultry, you're left with a lovely stock for soups and sauces.

If you like the 'roasted look' to a meat dish, but don't want to cook it completely in the oven, try bringing the dish to the boil on your hob, simmer for three-quarters of its cooking time, then finish it off in a hot oven in a lidded casserole, removing the lid for the last 15 minutes of cooking. Using this method you get both a soft texture and a 'golden' finish.

ESSENTIALS FOR THE FRIDGE AND STORE CUPBOARD

Here is my list of essentials. Depending on the space you have available, it may not be possible to store everything on this list. If this is the case, be selective and use it as a basis for choosing and storing everyday requirements. These essentials will help you create wonderful patés, dips and spreads, soups, food garnishes, salads, nibble-anytime snacks and light-meals. Everything on this list is healthy and nourishing!

Fresh Food Basics
(Fruit and Vegetables)

(All fresh food should keep 7-10 days in the fridge)

Apples
Aubergines
Avocados
Bananas
Beetroot (cooked)
Bean Sprouts
Blackberries
Blueberries
Broccoli
Carrots
Celery
Corn (baby and large cob)
Cucumber
Eggs (hard-boiled, yolks removed)
Fennel
Grapefruit
Kiwi Fruit
Lemons
Limes
Lettuce
Melons (of all kinds)
Mushrooms
Onions
Oranges
Pears
Peppers
Radishes
Raspberries
Spinach
Spring Onions
Strawberries
Tomatoes

Dairy Products

Milk (skimmed or semi-skimmed)
Low-Fat Spreads or Margarine
Cottage Cheese
Curd Cheese
Skimmed Milk soft cheese (Quark)
Fromage Frais
Edam, Gouda, Camembert*
*all have approx. 23% fat content, as opposed to Cheddar (30%) and Stilton (45%)
Yoghurt (low-fat or Greek)

Oils – Mustards – Sauces – Vinegars

Balsamic Vinegar
Corn Oil
Groundnut Oil
Mustard, English
Mustard, fresh grain
Olive Oil
Safflower Oil
Sesame Oil
Soya Sauce
Sunflower Oil
Tomato Ketchup
Tomato Purée (bottle or tube)
Vinegar, red wine
Vinegar, white wine
Walnut Oil
Worcestershire Sauce

Nuts – Pulses – Seeds

Perfect as an addition to casseroles and salads

Almonds (whole and flaked)
Barley
Broad Beans
Butter Beans
Caraway Seeds
Chick Peas
Cracked Wheat
Dried Peas
Fennel Seeds
Haricot Beans
Kidney Beans
Lentils
Pine Nuts
Pistachio Nuts (shelled)
Poppy Seeds
Walnuts (shelled)

Flours – Grains – Rice – Pasta

Basmati Rice
Bran
Brown Rice
Muesli (no added sugar)
Oatmeal
Oats, rolled

Pasta (including wholewheat varieties)
Rye Flour
Wheat Germ
Wheatmeal self-raising Flour
Wholemeal Flour
Wild Rice

Canned Foods

Anchovies
Artichokes
Asparagus
Baked Beans (sugar free)
Consommé (vegetable)
Corn (sugar free)
Salmon (red or pink)
Sardines
Tuna Fish
Tomato Purée
Tomatoes

Meat

Chicken (skinned first, then cooked – less fatty)
Turkey (skinned first, then cooked – less fatty)
Pork (optional, but must be lean)
Ham (optional, but must be lean)

Herbs – Bulbs – Roots

Fresh herbs are more plentiful and easily obtainable nowadays, so they should always be the preferred option; however dried herbs are perfectly acceptable for cooking if it's difficult to find the real McCoy

Basil
Chives
Coriander (fresh or seeds)
Dill
Garlic (bulb and powdered)
Ginger (root and powdered)

Herbs de Provence
Mint
Paprika
Parsley
Peppercorns (black)
Rosemary
Sage
Saffron
Turmeric

Breads

Supermarkets and bakeries stock a large range of healthy breads; just avoid any made with white flour

Granary
Pitta Bread (wholemeal)
Rye
Stoneground
Wholemeal

Dried Fruits

Apples
Apricots
Currants
Dates
Figs
Prunes
Raisins
Sultanas

Others

Greek Black Olives
Green Stuffed Olives
Honey
Sherry, dry
Sweeteners
Wine (dry white and red)

THE STOCK EXCHANGE

Gilt edged stocks are a great investment for some of the recipes featured in the F-F-F-Fizzical cookery book. And they give a great return.

Before you invest, take some sound advice: firstly, ingredients should always go into cold water and whilst cooking, the stock should be skimmed regularly with a slotted spoon – about every 10 minutes. The secret of a good stock is slow and gentle simmering. Also, don't put salt into a stock while it is cooking – add it later when preparing the dish requiring the stock. Important: home-made stock won't last longer than about 3-5 days in the fridge. However, it does freeze well.

CHICKEN STOCK

1 whole chicken carcass
1 large onion, peeled and quartered
2 carrots, peeled and chopped
1 stick celery, sliced into 4 pieces
1 bouquet garni
6 black peppercorns

Put the carcass in a large saucepan, cover it with cold water and bring to the boil. Remove scum with slotted spoon, half-cover with lid and simmer very gently for about 1½-2 hours. Add the other ingredients and continue simmering for another 1½-2 hours. Add cold water if the level drops below that of the bones. The liquid should reduce to half the original quantity. Remove from heat and strain. When cool, put into fridge. Within a couple of hours, as the stock chills, you'll find that all the fat rises to the top of the stock and is easily removed with a spoon.

FISH STOCK

1/2 kg (1 lb) fish heads, bones, tails, spines
1 large onion, peeled and quartered
1 stick celery, sliced into 4 pieces
2-3 parsley sprigs
1 bay leaf
6 black peppercorns

Put fish trimmings into a large saucepan, cover with water – maximum 1 litre (1¾ pt) – and stir in the remaining ingredients. Bring to boil, skimming off scum with a slotted spoon. Lower heat, cover pan and simmer for about 30-40 minutes. Skim regularly. Strain and reduce to two-thirds of original quantity by boiling rapidly. Strain, cool and refrigerate.

VEGETABLE STOCK

1 large onion, chopped
1 large carrot, chopped
1 large leek, chopped
1 large celery stick, cut into 4 pieces
8-10 spinach leaves
3-4 cabbage leaves
3-4 parsley stalks
2 bay leaves
6 black peppercorns
1 cup of dry white wine
570 ml (1 pt) water

In a large saucepan, place half the water then add all the vegetables and cook gently for about 7-8 minutes until they soften. Add the remaining ingredients along with the rest of the water, bring to the boil, then simmer for 30-35 minutes until the liquid is reduced by half. Strain through a sieve (press hard to remove liquid), discard pulp, and allow to cool then refrigerate.

BEEF STOCK

I tend to avoid red meat because it is high in fat and cholesterol; however if you are frantic for that flavour, use Oxo cubes or beef extracts such as Marmite or Bovril for the basis of a beef-flavoured stock.

'Come on and move it
You gotta groove it
You gotta shake it
and break it up
Come on and burn it
Go on and turn it ...'

From 'Get Up and Go!'
Margolis/Clayton

Lady Taverners Strawberry and
Mint Champagne

ACT ONE

KICK OFF WITH A COCKTAIL

Cocktails, for me, sum up celebration: of family, friends and life itself. I use the word cocktail in a non-generic sense, as in this first chapter you'll find cocktails for all occasions, any time of the day, every time of the day.

One of my great pleasures is filling a huge basket with mixed fresh fruit and vegetables. Whether on my kitchen or dining table, it's a feast for the eyes – an exotic mixing together of colours, strengths, power and energy foods that I love. For these are the most natural things we can pump into our bodies. They feed the blood, stimulate the heart and mind. Energise us!

Energy and stamina are all important for performers, none more so that me when I appear in a musical or pantomime – theatre's equivalent of the Olympics! I well remember a long-running show in Manchester. On the bill was a sensational acrobatic troupe, The Rastellis. It was a family act: Papa and five huge, handsome, hunky sons. Mama came too with her portable cooking ring. She whipped up a storm between shows, insisting on 'proper nutritioni for-a my boys!' and that 'onless-a they are-a fed-a well-a, they could-a nott-a perform-a at peaky!' She was a-right. The idea for canny cocktails came from my recollections of Mama Rastelli. A MEAL IN A GLASS! With her makeshift bain-marie Mama would heat up a mix of Marsala wine and beaten egg yolk with generous handfuls of sugar – Zabaglione. Her high-power hand whisking could be heard all over the theatre.

Now, of course, we have to ration egg yolk and sugar intake but the principle of nutrition in a cocktail is great to work on and infuses energy. It is also a healthy way of sharing social drinking.

Instead of Mama's cooking ring, I always carry a portable blender/liquidiser with me when I'm away from home.Backstage, in seconds, this super-speed device opens the door to an exciting array of powerful tastes, supplying instant vigour, nourishment and – let's not forget – sheer taste pleasure, all with a minimum of fuss and a maximum of f-f-f-fizz! What follows are my favourite cocktail recipes, fusing together the tang of Caribbean fruits with the goodness of traditional British ingredients. You will find these blends create a unique range of sensations to tease your taste buds and elevate your energy levels. Okay, let's celebrate!

Curtain up, light the lights...

- FRUIT COCKTAILS -

(All recipes approximately 2-3 servings)

The emphasis here is on fresh fruits blended to perfection, creating mouth-watering cocktails which will provide energy and delight throughout the whole day. And do remember, always wash fruit before preparing it.

FOUR FRUIT FANTASY

A refreshing breakfast drink or pick-me-up at any time.

570 ml (1 pt) chilled, unsweetened pineapple juice
1 orange, peeled and quartered
1 banana, peeled and halved
1 pear, peeled, cored and sliced

Blend all ingredients for 30 seconds, serve with ice cubes.

STRAWBERRY FIZZICAL

You may have to double the quantity of this one. Children, in particular, will come back for more.

225 g (8 oz) fresh strawberries (thawed from frozen are fine, too)

150 ml (¼ pt) fresh orange juice
15 g (1 tbsp) fresh lemon juice
15 g (1 tbsp) honey (or equivalent sweetener)
1 500 ml bottle chilled soda water
6 ice cubes

Blend strawberries, orange juice, lemon juice and honey for 15 seconds. Add ice and blend for a further 15 seconds. Pour into four glasses and top up with soda water. Float a strawberry on top of each glass and serve.

APRICOT ANGEL

Creamy, golden and utterly more-ish. Remember to soak the apricots in the milk overnight.

570 ml (1 pt) semi-skimmed or skimmed milk
225 g (8 oz) dried apricots (soaked in the
  milk overnight)
30 g (2 tbsp) low-fat yoghurt
10 g (2 tsp) honey (or equivalent sweetener)
Pinch of nutmeg

Blend all ingredients for 30-45 seconds. Serve in chilled glasses with an additional sprinkling of freshly grated nutmeg on top.

EARL GREY'S COOL MINT

This is a perfect all-summer drink.

570 ml (1 pt) of cooled Earl Grey tea,
made from leaves and strained
2 sprigs of fresh mint
10 ml (2 tsp) of freshly squeezed lime
or satsuma juice
10 ml (2 tsp) honey (or equivalent sweetener)
1 (2") strip of lemon peel
6 ice cubes

Set aside half the tea in a jug with the ice cubes. Blend mint, lime or satsuma juice, honey, lemon peel and remaining half of the tea for 15 seconds, then pour into the jug. Decorate glasses with a sprig of mint before serving.

BANANA CREAM WHIZ

We all know how good bananas are for our health; rich in fibre and practically a meal in themselves.

2 bananas, peeled and chopped
570 ml (1 pt) semi- or skimmed milk
Small pot low-fat natural yoghurt
10 ml (2 tsp) honey (or equivalent sweetener)
½ tsp powdered ginger
Cinnamon
6 ice cubes

Blend all ingredients, except cinnamon, for 30 seconds. Sprinkle a good pinch of cinnamon on top before serving. Alternatively, include cinnamon in the mixture and sprinkle ginger on top.

FOUR BERRY FIZZ

Some of the berries included here are seasonal but you can substitute with frozen when necessary. Loganberries make a good alternative but you may have to search for them. Either way, this is simply delightful.

570 ml (1 pt) unsweetened cranberry juice
100 g (4 oz) blackberries
100 g (4 oz) blueberries
100 g (4 oz) raspberries
275 ml (½ pt) sparkling or soda water
6 ice cubes
Black cherries for garnish

Wash the berries if fresh, then blend all ingredients, except water, for 30 seconds. Drink as is, or add the sparkling water if you prefer this cocktail less thick. Garnish with two or three black cherries on a cocktail stick.

- SAVOURY COCKTAILS -

(All recipes approximately 2-3 servings)

These cocktails are designed expressly for those moments when you crave something a little spicy and more substantial, but at the same time refreshing and with an extra zing.

TOMATO and GINGER FRAPPÉ

Talking about zing, this is even better if you nibble on a stick of celery whilst enjoying it.

250 ml (approx ½ pt) chilled tomato juice
2 medium fresh tomatoes, skinned, plus
½ cup of water or 200 g (half a 400 g
14 oz tin) of tinned tomatoes
6 good slices of cucumber, unpeeled
10 g (2 tsp) grated fresh ginger
5 ml (1 tsp) of soy sauce
4 dashes Tabasco

Blend all ingredients for 30 seconds. Drink immediately.

BORSCHT BEVY

If you love beetroot, as I do, this is a great refresher.

3 large cooked and peeled beetroot
570 ml (1 pt) fresh vegetable stock (see page 25)
1 good stick chopped celery
1 good sized carrot, washed, topped, tailed and chopped but not peeled
1 bouquet garni
15 ml (1 tbsp) lemon or lime juice

Grate two beetroot (leave the third one aside), place in a pan with the stock, celery and carrots. Bring to the boil, then add the bouquet garni and freshly milled black pepper to taste. Cover and simmer for about 30 minutes. Strain into a jug, leave to cool, then stir in lemon or lime juice and chill for a minimum of 2 hours. Just before serving, place liquid into a blender, chop and add remaining beetroot and blend for 30 seconds. Drink immediately.

CARROT CONSOMMÉ COCKTAIL

So easy and so tasty!

1 400 g (14 oz) tin of chilled consommé
1 large carrot, washed, topped, tailed and chopped but not peeled
3-4 good sprigs of parsley
Freshly ground black pepper

Blend all ingredients for 30 seconds and enjoy.

YELLOW MELLOW

Sweet corn and yellow peppers (capsicum) make a lovely combination. Even the colour tempts the taste buds.

225 g (8 oz) frozen sweet corn
1 yellow pepper, seeded and chopped
150 ml (¼ pt) water
275 ml (½ pt) semi- or skimmed milk
1 g (¼ tsp) turmeric
10 ml (2 tsp) light soy sauce or Tabasco to taste

Gently bring corn and pepper to the boil in water. Add turmeric and cool. Put mixture into a blender, add milk and soy sauce (or Tabasco) and blend for 30-45 seconds. Drink immediately.

- FILLER COCKTAILS -

(All recipes approximately 2-3 servings)

Healthy, nourishing and refreshing, these savoury drinks are great if you have to skip a meal or you need a little extra energy during a stressful day.

THREE GREENS FANTASY

Three of the zingiest greens combined in a deliciously good-for-you savoury treat.

1 large leek, washed and chopped
225 g (8 oz) broccoli sprigs
 and stalks, washed
175 g (6 oz) spinach leaves, washed
275 ml (½ pint) semi- or skimmed milk
Small pot of low-fat natural yoghurt
15 g (1 heaped tbsp) peeled pistachio nuts
10 ml (2 tsp) light soy sauce

Bring leek and broccoli slowly to the boil in milk then simmer gently. Add spinach leaves and simmer for a further five minutes. Put mixture to one side and allow to cool. Place yoghurt, pistachios and soy sauce into blender, add cooled vegetable mixture and blend for 30-45 seconds. If you prefer to drink ice cold, add 3-4 ice cubes before blending.

AA ANONYMOUS (AVOCADO and APPLE)

A delicious combination. My favourite apples for this one are Granny Smiths.

1 avocado, peeled and chopped
1 Granny Smith apple, washed and cored but not peeled
15 ml (1 tbsp) lime juice
275 ml (½ pt) cloudy, unsweetened, chilled apple juice
2-3 sprigs fresh basil

Place all ingredients into blender and blend for 30-45 seconds. Add more apple juice if you prefer the drink less thick.

CUPPA ENERGY

This may sound bizarre but the taste will surprise you and it's ideal if you need to miss a meal.

425 ml (½ pint) apple juice
100 ml (4 fl oz) unsweetened pineapple juice
1 half carrot, sliced
1 small celery stalk, sliced
2 spinach leaves
½ ripe pear
½ peeled banana

2 tsp sultanas
2 parsley sprigs
4 ice cubes

Keep sultanas to one side. Begin blending ingredients and drop in sultanas through the lip opening whilst whisking (this is because their weight and small size allows them to sink below the blades if you insert them with the rest of the mixture) for 45 seconds. Serve immediately.

GRAPEFRUIT GLOW

Get up and glow, glow, glow!

1 whole yellow or pink grapefruit, peeled, pithed and cut into sections
110 g (4 oz) green seedless grapes
15ml (1 tbsp) whole or flaked almonds
275 ml (½ pt) freshly squeezed orange juice
Small pot of low-fat natural yoghurt
Finely chopped almonds for garnish
Honey (or equivalent sweetener) to taste

Blend grapefruit, grapes and almonds in a little of the orange juice for 20 seconds. Add remaining orange juice, yoghurt and sweetener, if required, and blend for a further 10 seconds. Sprinkle finely chopped almonds on top before drinking.

- NON-ALCOHOLIC COCKTAILS -

(All recipes approximately 2-3 servings)

COOL MAC

(Mint, Apple and Cranberry)

An all- year-round party favourite.

425 ml (¾ pt) unsweetened cranberry juice
275 ml (½ pt) of cloudy apple juice
6-8 sprigs of fresh mint

Blend ingredients for 10 seconds and serve over crushed ice.

COLA COOLER

Stoke up a Coke, get F-F-F-Fizzical and P-P-P-Pep up a Pepsi!

2 cans diet Pepsi (or other cola)
6 juicy oranges, freshly squeezed
2 slices fresh pineapple

Blend a little of the orange juice with the pineapple for 10 seconds, transfer to serving jug and top up with rest of juice and the cola. Pour into tumblers on to crushed ice.

CARIBBEAN CREME

All that's missing is blue sea, white sand and palm trees.

1 banana, peeled and chopped
15 ml (1 tbsp) lime juice
275 ml (½ pt) skimmed milk
15 g (1 tbsp) chopped walnuts
Finely crushed walnuts for garnish

Blend all ingredients for 30 seconds, serve in tumblers on crushed ice if desired, and garnish with crushed walnuts.

COCONUT AMOUR

A loving cup.

6-8 fresh strawberries
1 tin of chilled coconut milk
15 g (1 tbsp) desiccated coconut
5 g (1 tsp) ground ginger

Blend all ingredients for 30 seconds, serve in tumblers on crushed ice if desired and float two strawberry halves on top of each glass.

PINE HAZEL

The combination of yoghurt and hazel nuts is not a new idea. When you add the pineapple juice, however, be prepared for an amazing experience.

570 ml (1 pt) unsweetened pineapple juice
275 ml (½ pt) of low-fat natural yoghurt
25 g (1 oz) of crushed hazel nuts

Blend all ingredients for 30 seconds, serve immediately.

PRUNELLA

F-F-F-Fizz tale: (In the manner of Billy Connolly). So, these prunes wanted to change their image. Big Prune said, 'Let's go up to the Big Kitchen for marketing advice. I know people at Starchy & Starchy,' and off went Itty Bitty Prune and Big Prune to see the big cheese. Starchy & Starchy said, 'Listen, you prune, this could be an expensive campaign.' 'Yeah, right, well you can prune that for a start,' said Itty Bitty Prune. Then they went out prunely petulant, found a pub which served skimmed milk and got well soaked overnight. At last everyone blended and finally the prunes got profiled up - and this was the result.

8-10 dried prunes
425 ml (3/4 pt) semi- or skimmed milk
1 small tub of low-fat natural yoghurt
Honey or sweetener

Soak the prunes overnight in half of the milk in the fridge. When ready to prepare, add the rest of the milk and sweeten to taste. Blend all ingredients for 30 seconds, serve immediately.

- ALCOHOLIC COCKTAILS -

(All recipes approximately 2-3 servings, unless otherwise indicated)

RED WINE CUP

(Approximately 12 glasses) – In moderation, red wine is proven to be good for the heart, and oranges are rich in vitamin C. Ideal to warm heart and soul.

2 oranges
Cloves
2 bottles red wine (preferably Beaujolais or similar young red)
1 cinnamon stick
Red currants

Stud the oranges with cloves and bake in a moderate oven for about 20 minutes until golden in colour. Cut oranges into slices with a sharp knife and put into a pan with the wine, adding the cinnamon stick. Bring steadily to the boil then simmer gently for 5 minutes. Float red currants on top and serve heated from a punchbowl.

MULLED WINE and HONEY

(Approximately 10-12 glasses)

Winter and Christmas without mulled wine is like Master Whittington without his Richard.

2 bottles claret
570 ml (1 pt) boiling water
60 ml (4 tbsp) honey (lavender honey is superb)
2 sticks cinnamon
5 g (1 tsp) nutmeg
2½ g (½ tsp) allspice

Heat the claret nearly to boiling point, add boiling water, honey, cinnamon, nutmeg and allspice, simmer over a low heat for a few minutes. Serve heated from a punchbowl.

MANGO SPRITZER

FIZZTIP: Some people think mangoes are difficult to peel – and they're right. But there is a fool-proof method. Slice the fruit vertically down either side of the stone, then score the flesh diagonally, criss-crossing in both directions without cutting through the skin and simply turn each half inside out. The 'hedgehog' cubes can then be easily sliced off the skin.

1 bottle good quality, chilled white wine
1 mango, peeled and cubed
1 500 ml bottle chilled soda or sparkling water

Blend mango with a little sparkling water to pulp (about 5-10 seconds). Combine wine and remaining water in a jug. Place a teaspoon of the mango in a wine glass, top up with the wine and water mixture and stir with a swizzle stick.

CHAMPAGNE BLONDE

A lovely summer's evening drink, if ever there was one.

FIZZTIP: To peel peaches easily, soak for a couple of minutes in hot water.

3 peaches (white, if possible)
1 bottle champagne (or good sparkling wine)
Angostura bitters

Peel and cut peaches into sections and blend for 30 seconds. Half fill champagne flutes with the peaches, top up with champagne and add two or three dashes of Angostura bitters. Can be served over crushed ice if preferred.

LADY TAVERNERS STRAWBERRY and MINT CHAMPAGNE*

A perfect accompaniment to Sunday village cricket.

450 g (1 lb) strawberries
8-10 fresh mint leaves
1 bottle champagne (or good sparkling wine)

Blend strawberries and mint leaves with a little water for 30 seconds. Strain through a fine sieve. Half-fill champagne flutes with the mixture and top up with champagne. Garnish with a sprig of mint. Can be served over crushed ice if preferred.

* (Lord's and Lady Taverners, the charity giving young people, particularly those with special needs, a sporting chance).

BLUE HUE

Not only delicious but magnificent to look at. Watch the colour change dramatically as you add the wine. Very more-ish.

225 g (8 oz) fresh blueberries
2 egg whites
½ bottle good chilled white wine, Chardonnay or similar
4-6 ice cubes (optional)

Whisk egg whites in blender until frothy. Add blueberries and ice cubes (if desired) and blend for further 30 seconds. Transfer to jug, stir in wine and serve immediately.

GRAPE DIVINE

Too, too divine dah-lings with red or white wine. If choosing the former, use red seedless grapes; if the latter, green seedless grapes.

225 g (8 oz) seedless red grapes
½ bottle fruity red wine, e.g. a good Beaujolais
4-6 ice cubes (optional)

Blend grapes for 30-45 seconds (with ice if desired), transfer to jug, stir in wine and serve immediately.

Fizz-tale: This is a glory story about a pretty little Juicer that grew up to become a great Mixer with all the right equipment. She of course went to Hollywood, became a huge success at cocktail parties and we all know her now as Blender Jackson.

'The power inside is the ultimate ride
Get up! Don't sit! Get fit!
You gotta get up, get down-get up!
You've gotta step out, step up-step up,
Step out, step up-step up, step out!
F-f-f-fizzical! F-f-f-fizzical!'

From 'Get Up and Go!'
Margolis/Clayton

Chilled Smoked Trout with Yoghurt
and Orange Dressing

ACT TWO

FIZZICAL FAST FILLERS AND FOOD ON THE MOVE

In 1965 Burt Bacharach and Hal David wrote a song for me called 'London Life'. I also recorded their haunting 'Trains and Boats and Planes' and followed that with a Bacharach and David double album, recorded with the New World Symphony Orchestra. 'Trains and Boats' always reminds me of busy people with busy lives – rushing, running late, meetings and appointments here, there and everywhere, grabbing a quick bite when desperation beckons! The 'I'm starving!' syndrome.

FIZZTIP: Never shop when you're hungry.

Hunger makes us do silly things, particularly as we all live in an increasingly stressful world. This technological age can be exciting but it exacts a toll, unless we discipline our eating regime. 'DISCIPLINE? AAAaaaarrrgh!' I hear you groan, but soft – my light from yonder window says, 'give me a break!' Discipline is not that hard and it's worth it. A little forethought and preparation will help you to eat, live and play better. If this means a major re-think about those three bastions of survival in the kitchen: the store cupboard, the refrigerator and the bread bin – DO IT! Talking about discipline, one of the songs composed for Fizzical recommends:

'DO IT DURING LUNCH, DO IT AFTER WORK,
DO IT LATE AT NIGHT – BUT DO IT!
SHAPING UP IS NOT SO HARD TO DO
BUT IT CAN BE THE MAKING OF YOU
YOU'D BETTER BELIEVE IT!'*

So, sally forth with your favourite essentials: foods you can nibble at any time of the day or night, or imaginatively concoct into fillings and wholesome sandwiches, instant salads or nourishing pates and dips. You need to get serious about this. Allocate, and stick to, three hours a week to prepare your essentials, so that the fridge becomes a storehouse of feel-good energy and taste-great sustenance. Once you get into the swing of this routine, I swear you'll – and here come another three Fs: Feel, Fare and Function better, both physically and mentally.

FIZZTIP: Tupperware lunch box fills the bill) with three courses in it. A soup, main course, fruit and a bottle of still water.

Most workplaces now have microwave ovens, so you can heat up your food. If you're setting off on a long train journey, devise a meal box menu that's filling and practical. It should satisfy you so that an hour later

* From 'Do it!' by K.Clayton

you don't feel you have to cheat! (Familiar feeling?) Your box might comprise an avocado dip, cucumber slices, spring onions and carrot slivers. A well-filled wholemeal sandwich of Edam cheese, crunchy celery and tomato, or a rice or pasta dish. For dessert, a fresh pear and a banana, and of course some bottled water for drinking. Don't give a second thought to eating with your fingers or a fork. Just take a look around at the other passengers tucking into pre-packed soggy bacon burgers! Chances are that with the addition of a can of soft drink, a packet of salt and vinegar crisps plus a chocolate bar thrown in, they've paid a lot more for their sustenance – and they're paying heavily in health currency.

Your motto is, as Falstaff should have said, 'Begone bacon butty and hail healthburger!' (see Act Three p. 85). The travel-guzzler's meal on the wheel will return to say hello! a burp at a time. Your Fizzical travel box is the healthy ticket to ride!

- PATÉS, DIPS AND SPREADS -

I find it a good idea to keep about 4-6 small dishes of healthy dips, patés and spreads on hand in the fridge for a kick-start at any moment, a between-meal snack or when the door bell rings and friends drop in. Use part of your three-hours-a-week preparation time to make them up and also prepare vegetables and salads for dipping, stuffing and munching. You'll find it time well spent.

COTTAGE CHEESE and PILCHARD PATÉ

225 g (8 oz) tinned pilchards
55 g (2 oz) creamed low-fat cottage cheese
55 g (2 oz) low-fat or Greek yoghurt
¼ tsp grain mustard
Chopped chives
Juice of ¼ lemon

For a chunky paté, empty pilchards into a bowl, add the cheese, yoghurt, mustard, chives and lemon juice and mix well with a fork. A creamier paté is achieved by using a liquidiser. Garnish with olives and serve on toasted wholemeal bread.

CELERY STICKS with SMOKED MACKEREL PATÉ

1 smoked mackerel, filleted
55 g (2 oz) cottage cheese
55 g (2 oz) Greek yoghurt
1 spring onion, finely chopped
Juice of ¼ lemon wedge
(retain 3 remaining wedges)
Watercress
Cayenne pepper
3 celery sticks cut into thirds

Remove skin from the fish. Flake the fish and place it in a bowl then, using a fork, mix it with the cottage cheese, Greek yoghurt and lemon juice. If you prefer a creamier paté, use a liquidiser. When the mixture is blended, stir in the very finely chopped spring onion. Carefully spoon the mixture into the hollow of the celery sticks and, before serving, sprinkle a little cayenne pepper on top and garnish with watercress and the remaining lemon wedges. Perfect with wholemeal Melba toast.

AUBERGINE PATÉ with WHOLEMEAL MELBA TOAST

2 large aubergines
1 finely chopped medium red onion
30 ml (2 tbsp) olive or groundnut oil
15 g (1 tbsp) bran
5 g (1 tsp) wheat germ
6 chopped black olives
Juice of 1 lemon
Chopped parsley

Place aubergines on a baking tray and cook for about 30 minutes in a moderate to high oven. When soft, peel off the skins under cold running water. Place in a blender with all the ingredients but with only half the parsley and mix for 10-15 seconds. Sprinkle remaining parsley on top before serving. For the wholemeal Melba toast, lightly toast four slices of wholemeal bread in a toaster and, while hot, cut off the crusts and slice through each piece horizontally (creating two thin Melbas from each slice). Put the toast in a pre-heated oven and remove when golden brown (about 10-12 minutes).

AVOCADO DIP with LEMON and SPRING ONION

1 ripe avocado
1 chopped spring onion
15 ml (1 tbsp) freshly squeezed lemon juice
Chilli powder to taste
1 small tomato, washed, seeded
and chopped

Peel avocado, discard skin and stone, and using a food processor combine flesh, spring onion, lemon juice and chilli powder. Mix until smooth, transfer to a bowl and gently blend in the chopped tomato.

POTTED SALMON SPREAD

225 g (8 oz) cooked salmon,
skinned and boned
30-45 g (2-3 tbsp) cottage cheese
1 lemon (rind and juice)
10 g (2 tsp) finely chopped dill
15 g (1 tbsp) toasted flaked almonds, crushed
Salt and pepper to taste

Flake the salmon then place in a food processor or blender with the cottage cheese, lemon rind and juice, half of the dill and a little salt and pepper. Blend for 20-

25 seconds. Return mixture to bowl and fold in the crushed almonds. Pack mixture into ramekins, cover with Clingfilm and chill. Before serving, sprinkle the remaining dill on top.

CLIVE and CILLA DUNN'S PORTUGUESE PATÉ

Salty Algarve air; muted flurry of waves marching across the sweeping sand, filling the footprints of fishermen as they carry their catch from boat to beachside market...Cor, I drifted off there for a moment. Clive and Cilla Dunn, best friends for many a year, wine and dine it healthily in Portugal, along with their beautiful daughters Polly (a sensational Cordon Bleu chef) and Jessica (an outstanding painter). Clive and my Mike like to partake of a Portuguese paté made from sardines. This is my version of the Dunn recipe.

2 x120 g (4 oz) tins of sardines in oil
1 x 50 g (2 oz) tin of anchovies in oil
Juice of ½ lemon
30 g (2 tbsp) sun-dried tomatoes, chopped
30 g (2 tbsp) tomato purée
Freshly ground black pepper

Blend all the ingredients for 60 seconds in a blender or food processor; cool in fridge for a good hour before serving with Melba toast, crudités or low-fat savoury biscuits.

- SANDWICHES -

(All recipes serve one)

The sandwich: This unique British invention was created by the somewhat dodgy John Montagu, the 4th Earl of Sandwich. His other claim to fame was as First Lord of the Admiralty from 1771 to 1782. Sadly, our saucy sailor sandwich maker was not to be otherwise admired. In the American War of Independence his gormless generalship helped sink Britain's aspirations without trace. So next time you partake of a sandwich, remember it cost us America! However, without Johnny Sandwich, burgers might never have ended up between two buns, and think how messy that would be.

And while we are on sandwiches, you don't need me to tell you how to make one. Suffice it to say that now you have a larder full of essentials, you can be your own inventive earl. Here are some suggestions to encourage you to depart from the norm.

DELUXE SALAD SANDWICH

Fizz tip: Mayonnaise on a sandwich is beguiling but try this healthier alternative: Mayo Frais. Simply put into a small bowl ½ tsp of powdered mustard, 5ml/1 tsp of honey, 10ml/2 tsp of fromage frais and blend with a spoon. Slowly add 30ml/2 tbsp of olive oil, a little salt and pepper to taste, and you have a delicious spread to give any salad sandwich that little extra pizzazz. A traditional shop-bought salad sandwich usually comprises of limp lettuce, wilted cucumber and razor-blade thin tomato slices embalmed in butter. Taste the difference when you really go to town blending your own fresh salad ingredients. For example:

Endive, sliced fennel, sweet corn kernels and Italian tomato slices (good and thick!) with fresh basil.

Grated carrot, sliced celery, Lolo Rosso lettuce, beetroot and chopped spring onions.

Avocado, apple slices, sultanas and spinach leaves.

Sliced banana, toasted flaked almonds, sliced radish and cottage cheese.

Tomato, thinly sliced onion, cold cooked petit-pois (sounds silly, but it's delish!) and finely chopped mint.

Finely sliced red pepper, chopped celery, raisins and a few walnut pieces – a savoury/sweet crunch you'll love.

Sliced banana, apple and kiwi fruit with a sprinkling of cinnamon – voilà, a fruit salad sandwich!

TWO-TIER CHICKEN SALAD SANDWICH with FLAKED ALMONDS

FIZZTIP: Thinly slice a red onion – less fiery than its white sister – and place into a small bowl, add a teaspoon of honey and cover with red wine vinegar. Seal with Clingfilm and leave to marinate overnight. The onion softens, becomes more easily digestible and less detectable on the breath. Hey Presto! you have a tangy and crunchy addition to any sandwich. The marinating onion will keep for a good 7-10 days in the fridge.

So, for this sandwich, start with three wholemeal bread slices sparingly covered with a low-fat spread. The first layer contains a generous portion of sliced chicken breast meat with sliced tomato and shredded lettuce. For the second layer add sliced avocado, the marinated onion and flaked almonds. If you want more moisture, a sprinkle of olive or walnut oil or mayo frais (see p.58) works well. This is one of my all-time favourite sandwiches.

TWO-TIER PLOUGHMAN'S SANDWICH with EDAM and PICKLED RED ONION

As above, take three wholemeal bread slices, add low-fat spread, fill first layer with several slices of low-fat Edam and a leaf or two of lettuce. On the next layer add a generous amount of marinated onion (see above) and some finely chopped celery. Take it on a train journey and watch the other passengers turn green with envy!

RED SALMON, CUCUMBER and GREEN PEPPER SANDWICH

Finely chop the cucumber and green pepper, mix with enough red salmon to make a generous wholemeal sandwich. The finishing touch requires stirring a generous helping of cottage cheese into the mixture. Add a dash of Tabasco and a few chopped chives. A taste triumph.

- SNACKS -

(All recipes approximately 3-4 persons)

CHILLED SMOKED TROUT with YOGHURT and ORANGE DRESSING

Remember that trout has a high fatty acid content and is therefore very good for you. Another plus is that it's comfortably filling and not expensive.

4 skinned and filleted smoked trout
Finely grated rind and juice of 1 orange
150 ml (¼ pint) natural yoghurt
Finely shredded spinach leaves for serving
Orange segments to garnish

Cover and chill trout fillets for 30 minutes. Combine orange juice, rind and yoghurt in a bowl, seasoning with freshly ground pepper. Spread spinach on four serving plates, place a fillet on each plate and spoon over the dressing; garnish with orange segments. (If preferred spinach can be cooked and chilled).

GRAVLAX with MINT and DILL DRESSING

Gravlax is pickled salmon – Swedish style. I love it – especially with the combination of fresh dill and mint.

15 g (1 tbsp) grain mustard
75 ml (3 fl oz) olive oil
15 ml (1 tbsp) white wine vinegar
15 g (1 tbsp) fresh chopped dill
15 g (1 tbsp) fresh chopped mint
900 g (2 lb) Gravlax

Mix the mustard, oil, vinegar, dill and mint. Keep overnight in fridge to allow dressing to blend. Lay thin slices of Gravlax on four serving plates and pour dressing over each portion. Garnish with a little chopped dill and mint.

SPRING VEGETABLE CRUDITÉS with GREEK YOGHURT DIP

Refreshing and light, perfect between main meals.

2 celery stalks, trimmed and cut into eight sticks
1 green pepper, halved, seeded and cut into strips
4 baby corn, sliced lengthways into eight pieces
1 carrot, cut into julienne sticks
4 cherry tomatoes
8 mange tout

For the dip:

1 cup of Greek yoghurt
2 minced garlic cloves
15 ml (1 heaped tbsp) chopped spring onions
10 ml (2 tsp) Greek honey
Dash of Tabasco

Prepare the vegetables and mix together the dip ingredients. Serve on a large platter with the dip-bowl as the centrepiece.

HOUMMUS STUFFED CHERRY TOMATOES (or EGGS)

Fizz-tale: Hoummus always brings back memories of my trips to Greece, in particular a concert performance with Kenny Clayton and his trio on the shores of the Vouliagmeni Lake. Our backdrop – 100 foot-high cliffs with diners' tables set around the clear waters - a magical setting with magic musicians. We dumped the bousouki in the lake, gave them some Jazz-a-ma-tazz and ouzo'd on down the road!

For this classic dish, uncooked chick peas are best, but if you're in a hurry, use tinned.

225 g (8 oz) chick peas or 225g (8 oz) tinned chick peas
2 cloves garlic, crushed
30 ml (4 tbsp) olive oil
Juice of 2 lemons
10 g (2 tsp) ground cumin
Cayenne pepper
Salt to taste
150 g (5 oz) Tahina paste (optional)
12-15 cherry tomatoes (or 10-12 hard-boiled eggs with yolks removed and sliced in half)
Olive oil
Freshly chopped parsley

First, we need to make the hoummus – and there are

two ways to do this: 1) the two hour method or, 2) the fast-track version. Option 1 is to put the chick peas into a pan of boiling salted water and soak for two hours, followed by gentle cooking for about 90 minutes. Option 2 is to use tinned chick peas which merely need to be heated. Whichever method you choose, continue thus: drain, reserving the liquid. When coolish, put chick peas, garlic, olive oil, lemon juice, cumin and a pinch of cayenne pepper into a blender and blend for about 15-20 seconds. Taste and add salt if necessary. Blend once more, adding just enough of the liquid to make the mixture into a smooth, creamy paste. You may add Tahina paste at this stage if desired. Slice off the top of the cherry tomatoes, scoop out flesh and fill with the hoummus; or, likewise, fill the halved, cooked eggs. Finally, sprinkle the whole with a little olive oil and garnish with the parsley.

CHILLED CAULIFLOWER GRATIN

Say cheese and smile in classic style.

12 cauliflower florets
1 cup of low-fat natural yoghurt or fromage frais
45 g (3 heaped tbsp) finely grated low-fat Edam cheese
Salt and black pepper to taste
Cayenne pepper or paprika

If you have a steamer, steam the florets for 7-8 minutes until cooked but not soggy. Alternatively, bring to the boil in a little water and simmer for 5-6 minutes. Let florets cool and put into fridge for an hour. Then arrange on a serving dish. Mix together half the grated cheese with the yoghurt and pour it over the cauliflower. Sprinkle on remainder of the cheese and add salt and freshly ground black pepper. Or you could sprinkle a little cayenne pepper or paprika for extra colour and bite.

- SALADS -

FIZZTIP: Pasta and Rice. Adding 1 tbsp of olive oil to boiling water prevents pasta and rice sticking.

BROWN RICE, CORN and WALNUT SALAD

Another high-fibre filler with a genuinely crunchy texture.

225 g (8 oz) brown rice
2 spring onions
1 red pepper, finely chopped
340 g (11 oz) tin of sweet corn kernels
(drained) or cooked frozen corn
30 g (2 tbsp) bran
30 g (2 tbsp) chopped walnut pieces
50 g (2 oz) chopped stoned dates

For the dressing:

30 ml (2 tbsp) corn oil or similar
30 ml (2 tbsp) unsweetened apple juice
15 ml (1 tbsp) white wine vinegar
5 g (1 tsp) curry powder
Freshly ground black pepper

Put rice in plenty of boiling water. Return to a medium boil for approximately 30 minutes or until tender. Drain under cold water and leave to one side until cool. Mix together the rice with the salad ingredients, then shake the dressing ingredients in a jar, and just before serving pour over the rice mix and toss thoroughly.

PASTA SALAD with FENNEL, PEARS and PINK SALMON

An unbeatable combination: the unique aniseed flavour of fennel, the succulence of fresh pear, the lightness and colour of pink salmon – and the soft texture of pasta. Pasta-fazool!

175 g (6 oz) pasta spirals
350 g (12 oz) tin of pink salmon, drained, boned and flaked
½ a fennel, finely sliced
1 large pear, peeled and cut into small chunks
1 red pepper, de-seeded and finely chopped
4 black olives, stoned and sliced
Freshly ground black pepper
Olive oil
Balsamic vinegar

Cook pasta in a large pan of boiling water until tender; drain and cool. In a large glass salad bowl (it looks prettier) mix pasta and all the ingredients gently. Serve on individual plates with a little olive oil, a few drops of balsamic vinegar and ground pepper.

PESTO PASTA SALAD with FRESH BASIL

This recipe contains Parmesan cheese which, unfortunately, has a high-fat content. However, it calls for only very little and you simply cannot have pesto without Parmesan so, on this occasion only, indulge yourself! This dish is perfect as a hot starter or eaten cold as a summer salad.

225 g (8 oz) macaroni (or penne)
Grated low-fat Edam cheese
Few sprigs fresh basil

For the pesto sauce:

50 g (2 oz) fresh basil leaves
15 g (1 tbsp) pine kernels
90 ml (6 tbsp) olive oil
1 crushed garlic clove
25 g (1 oz) grated Parmesan cheese
Ground black pepper

Boil the pasta in plenty of hot water (timing will depend on whether the pasta is fresh or dried). When tender, rinse in cold running water and put aside. Whilst the pasta is cooking, grate the Edam and set aside. Put all the ingredients for the pesto sauce – except the Parmesan – into a blender and mix until smooth (10-15 seconds). Transfer to bowl, mix in the Parmesan then gently stir sauce into the pasta. Sprinkle the Edam on top and finish off with a few fresh basil leaves.

COMBINATION FRESH and DRIED FRUIT SALAD with YOGHURT

This is a little creation you can enjoy as a salad or, leaving out the juice and yoghurt, as a topping for breakfast muesli.

150 ml (¼ pint) unsweetened apple juice
Juice of half a lemon
110 g (4 oz) strawberries
110 g (4 oz) raspberries
110 g (4 oz) black cherries, stoned
50 g (2 oz) stoned prunes, chopped
50 g (2 oz) dried apricots, chopped
50 g (2 oz) dried figs, chopped
30-45 ml (2-3 tbsp) Greek yoghurt
25 g (2 oz) toasted almond flakes

Blend together the apple and lemon juice in a small jug. In a bowl, mix together all fruits, pour liquid over and chill for at least an hour. Serve with a dollop of yoghurt and sprinkle almonds on top.

SAVOURY LETTUCE PARCELS

This is one of several snack ideas I collected on a tour of the Far East with Sir Harry Secombe – a Knight to remember.

1 medium chicken breast, cut into thin slivers
50 g (2 oz) cooked brown rice
1 small onion, finely chopped
5 ml (1 tsp) soy sauce
5 ml (1 tsp) red wine vinegar
5 ml (1 tsp) dry sherry
5 ml (1 tsp) honey (or sweetener)
4 sturdy Iceberg lettuce leaves

Cook chicken slivers slowly in a non-stick pan for about 6-7 minutes. Add other ingredients, except lettuce leaves, and stir for about 5 minutes. Put one lettuce leaf on each plate, divide mixture between them, wrap leaves around filling and eat immediately. Fingers permitted.

YOGHURT POTATO SALAD with CHICKEN (or TURKEY) and CHIVES

Potato salad is a good, reliable standby as an 'additional' rather than a main dish. However, this jazzed-up version has some interesting 'extras' and can be enjoyed as either a snack or main course.

700 g (1½ lbs) small new potatoes
2 cooked chicken breasts (or 1 turkey breast) cut into cubes
5 g (1 tsp) English mustard
5 ml (1 tsp) white wine
25 g (1oz) finely chopped red onion
30 ml (2 tbsp) Greek yoghurt (or French fromage frais)
1 finely chopped celery stick
5-6 chopped chives

Cook unpeeled potatoes in boiling water until tender then drain. Mix mustard with white wine. When potatoes have cooled, slice into a mixing bowl. Add chicken cubes, onion and chopped celery. Over this mixture, pour the mustard and wine dressing. Finally, add the yoghurt and chopped chives; mix gently. Add a few more chopped chives for garnish.

SALMON CUCUMBER and SPRING ONION SALAD

Serve on wholemeal bread as an open sandwich, as a filling for hot jacket potatoes or on its own.

400 g (14 oz) tin of red salmon, drained and bones removed
½ medium cucumber, thinly sliced
5-6 spring onions, finely chopped
15 g (1 tbsp) chopped parsley
15 ml (1 tbsp) olive oil
5 ml (1 tsp) lemon juice
Freshly ground black pepper

Using a fork, gently mix all ingredients together in a bowl and, before serving, add freshly ground black pepper to taste.

ROAST VEGETABLE SALAD

This is a versatile main dish or a wonderful addition to barbecues, summer party menus or as a snack whenever the mood takes you. And it couldn't be simpler – or quicker – to prepare!

1 carrot, peeled and cut into thick matchstick shapes
1 stick celery, cut into chunky bite-size pieces

1 parsnip, peeled and cut into thick matchstick shapes
1 medium onion, peeled and cut into rings
10-12 French beans, washed but left whole
1 head of broccoli, cut into small florets
Olive oil
75 g (3 oz) button mushrooms, washed but left whole
Salt and freshly ground black pepper
15 g (1 heaped tbsp) chopped walnut pieces
Balsamic vinegar

Pre-heat oven to 180C/450F/gas mark 4. Place all the vegetables except the mushrooms into a heat-proof casserole or roasting pan. Sprinkle olive oil generously over the vegetables (but don't drown them) and with a wooden spoon, gently stir the contents, making sure that all the vegetables are coated with the oil. Roast in pre-heated oven, uncovered, for about 15 minutes, then stirring all the while add the mushrooms and continue cooking for another 10 minutes. Let cool and refrigerate until ready to serve. Before serving, add salt and pepper to taste and sprinkle walnut pieces on top. Finally, a few drops of balsamic vinegar will add that special zing.

'When they see you thinner
They'll know that you're
a Winner
Get up and go right now!'

From 'Get Up and Go!'
Margolis/Clayton

Breakfast Pancakes with
Smoked Salmon

ACT THREE

BOUNTIFUL BREAKFASTS AND BONA BRUNCHES

Breakfast conjures up different images to different people. For some, it's about grabbing a bite before dashing off to work, for mums or housewives, chances are it's a slice of toast or a cup of tea. However there can't be many of us who don't look forward to a luxurious breakfast or Sunday morning brunch while wrestling with the Sunday papers.

I generally start the day around 7.00 a.m. (filming days earlier by two or three hours) with a cup of Twining's delicious English Breakfast Tea, then go straight into my morning FIZZICAL WORKOUT, followed by a bowl of muesli or bran flakes with half-fat or skimmed milk, or a glass of my Cuppa Energy (see p. 38). However, when family or friends come around for a late breakfast or brunch, especially either of my big brothers who love to binge on breakfast, I go to town Victorian style – sideboard overflowing, a veritable feast of breakfast dishes, fresh fruit, exotic juices, an assortment of oats and brans, smoked salmon and choices of kedgeree, sweet and savoury breakfast burgers, cholesterol-free omelettes (yes, and they taste great!), piping hot porridge, warmed tomatoes, onions and mushrooms with coriander as well as an array of whole grain breads, rolls and toasted muesli. I know – it's positively decadent, my dears!

Make it easy on yourself with a little pre-prep the night before. Chop all the dried fruits and veg; grate, or use your blender to make, bread crumbs then cover and refrigerate; make muesli loaf (see p. 93) or toasted muesli (see p. 84); cook rice for the kedgeree and prepare the fish stock (if you have some already frozen, remove to thaw). Why not even lay the table? Then in the morning, 45 minutes is all you'll need to rustle up a bountiful breakfast spread to really kick-start everyone's day. Have the smell of freshly ground coffee wafting through the house (find a great decaffeinate). Coffee aroma tempts the taste buds, so make it ready to coincide with the start of the meal.

For those of you on the move, remember that you now have a store cupboard, fridge and bread bin full of essentials that can be integrated into your feast. We need to take the bitchin' out of the kitchen! Planning, preparation, production and presentation of good, healthy food must not be a chore. Treat it as a workout.

I had some wonderful working times with Eric Morecambe and Ernie Wise. Their famous kitchen sketch, choreographed by Ernest Maxin, in which toasting, whisking and grapefruit slicing become a hilarious delight, is the general idea. Dance while you're dishing. Your guests will be a-mazed!

Fresh, colourful ingredients, loving care taken over the look of the finished dishes and some attention to the atmosphere you create. Sit back, take the applause and enjoy your pause.

- BREAKFASTS IN A GLASS -

(All recipes serve 2-3 persons)

Running late? No time to sit and contemplate? Try one of these breakfasts in a glass. They're packed with energy and will set you up for the morning.

SAVOURY CELERY and WALNUT WINTER WARMER

425 ml (½ pt) semi-skimmed milk
2 large celery sticks, washed and cut into 2.5cm (1") lengths
30 g (2 tbsp) chopped walnuts
30 g (2 tbsp) roughly chopped mixed fresh herbs (e.g. parsley, chives, basil and oregano)
2½ ml (½ tsp) Worcestershire sauce

While warming half a pint of the milk in a pouring saucepan, blend all the other ingredients with the remaining milk in a blender for about 25 seconds. Add this mixture to the saucepan and when hot, but not boiling, pour into drinking mugs. If you want to spice it up, add a dollop of yoghurt on top and finish off with a sprinkling of cayenne pepper.

FRESH FRUIT and NUT BRAN with YOGHURT

1 large banana, peeled and cut in two
1 large fresh pear, peeled, cored and quartered
1 kiwi fruit, peeled and quartered
15 g (1 tbsp) of bran
15 g (1 tbsp) flaked almonds
570 ml (1 pt) low-fat natural yoghurt
Wheat germ, for topping

Put all ingredients into a blender and mix until smooth (about 15-20 seconds). Pour into individual glasses and sprinkle on a little wheat germ.

PRUNE, FIG and FRESH ORANGE JUICE

6-8 dried prunes
6-8 dried figs
570 ml (1 pt) freshly squeezed orange juice
275 ml (½ pt) low-fat plain yoghurt
Nutmeg or cinnamon, to taste

Put all ingredients into a blender and mix until smooth (about 15-20 seconds). Pour into individual glasses and sprinkle a little nutmeg or cinnamon on top.

- BOUNTIFUL BREAKFASTS AND BONA BRUNCHES -

(All recipes 3-4 good servings)

APRICOT, PRUNE and RAISIN PORRIDGE

'You cannot be serious!' yelped my husband when I first used him as a guinea pig for this invention; now he's hooked. Though this 'breakthrough' may cause grave offence to traditional Scots porridge-ists, it is absolutely delicious. So, to all north of the border, 'lang may yer' lum reek wi the skirl o' the heiland prune and raisin spoon dance.'

100 g (4oz) coarse oatmeal (or rolled oats)
5 g (1 tsp) salt
1 litre (1¾ pints) water
6-8 dried apricots, chopped
6-8 dried prunes, chopped
15-30 g (1-2 tbsp) raisins

Put oatmeal (or oats) into a pan, add salt and water, bring slowly to the boil stirring occasionally to prevent sticking. When mixture thickens turn down heat to simmer for about 15 minutes, then add apricots, prunes and raisins. Simmer for a further 5 minutes, then serve.

KEDGEREE with SWEET CORN

It may be considered sacrilege to use any fish other than smoked haddock in kedgeree, and that's fine, but for extra goodness, try it with smoked mackerel. Either way, it's Fizzically good for you and wonderfully tasty!

500 g (1lb) cooked smoked haddock
(or mackerel) fillets
175 g (6 oz) brown long grain rice
1 finely chopped large onion
350 g (12 oz) corn kernels, tinned or
cooked from frozen
15 ml (1 tbsp) vegetable oil
10 g (2 tsp) curry powder
5 ml (1 tsp) lemon juice
570 ml (1 pt) clear fish stock (see p. 24)
2 bay leaves
30 g (2 tbsp) chopped parsley
Ground black pepper
1 lemon (for garnish)

Remove skin and any bones from the fish, flake it, set to one side. In frying pan cook the onion in oil for 3-4 minutes, stirring occasionally. Add the curry powder, cook for a further 2 minutes then put in the uncooked rice and lemon juice. Make sure rice is well-coated with the liquid and stir for a further 3-4 minutes.

Slowly pour on the stock, add the pepper and bay leaves, bring to the boil then turn down to simmer, without stirring, for about 35-40 minutes. Stir in fish and corn, continue cooking for a further 10 minutes or until liquid has been absorbed. Finally, remove bay leaves, stir in parsley and turn into a heated serving dish. Garnish with lemon quarters.

TOASTED MUESLI

There are a number of no-added-sugar mueslis available in supermarkets and health food stores; or make your own following this simple recipe: 6 parts rolled oats, to 2 parts bran flakes plus 1 part wheat germ and 1 part bran. The following recipe is for 3-4 people.

30 ml (2 tbsp) honey or equivalent sweetener
10 ml (2 tsp) vegetable oil
50 g (2oz) mixed chopped nuts
150 g (5oz) muesli mix
Mixed chopped dried fruits

Pre-heat oven to 180C/350F/gas mark 4. Gently warm honey in a small pan until it bubbles then remove pan from heat. Add oil, nuts and stir in muesli. Spread mixture onto a greased baking tray and bake for about 20 minutes, stirring occasionally to allow all-over browning. Cool on the tray. Serve with chopped fruit on top.

SAVOURY BREAKFAST BURGER

Here is a breakfast-brightening savoury burger that works wonderfully served on a wholemeal bap.

3 egg whites
1 cup of thinly diced chicken, pork, or fish
1 small onion, chopped
½ cup mushroom, chopped
5 ml (1 tsp) vegetable oil or margarine
½ tsp soy sauce
15 g (1 tbsp) shelled pistachio nuts

Put egg whites into a bowl. In a non-stick pan with the oil and soy sauce, gently fry onion and chicken (or pork or fish) for about 5-6 minutes. Add mushrooms and pistachios and fry for a further 2-3 minutes. Put ingredients into the bowl with the egg whites, mix gently, and using the same pan which should be on simmering, spoon the mixture 1 tablespoon at a time. Fry for about 3 minutes, turning at least once. For a thicker burger, use an egg ring with 2 tablespoons of the mixture, but allow a little more cooking time.

SWEET BREAKFAST BURGER

Ah, sweet burger of life at last I've found you...

3 egg whites
30 ml (2 tbsp) low-fat milk
45 g (3 tbsp) All Bran
30 g (2 tbsp) muesli
15 g (1 tbsp) sultanas
8 chopped dried apricots
15 ml (1 tbsp) honey or equivalent sweetener

Mix all ingredients in a bowl. When thoroughly blended, put mixture into the fridge for 30 minutes. Into a non-stick pan that has been pre-heated and set at simmering, put separate heaped tablespoons of the mixture. Cook for about 3 minutes – or until dark, golden brown – turning at least once. Place in a heated serving dish and serve immediately. Alternatively, serve cold with a little yoghurt and honey. For a thicker burger, use an egg ring with 2 tablespoons of the mixture, but allow a little more cooking time.

TRICOLORE OMELETTE

This takes its name from the Italian flag and its three colours of red, green and white. The recipe is dedicated to the Three Tenors, better known as the World Cup Wanderers.

- 4 egg whites
- 1 beef tomato cut and diced into small pieces (leave skin on)
- 1 green pepper, stalk-removed, seeded, cut and diced into small pieces
- 1 small tub of cottage cheese
- 15 g (1 tbsp) fresh basil, or 5 g (1 tsp) of dried basil
- Freshly ground black pepper

Mix all ingredients in a bowl, then pour into a heated non-stick frying pan with a little oil. Cook for 3-4 minutes, turn, and when cooked serve immediately or let it cool and serve cold with a green salad.

BREAKFAST PANCAKES with SMOKED SALMON

Here is a blini fit for a genie; an Arabian nights dish to add magic to your morning.

100 g (4 oz) wholemeal flour
275 ml (½ pint) semi-skimmed milk
3 egg whites
Pinch of salt
4-6 slices of smoked salmon
5 ml (1 tsp) lemon juice
Greek yoghurt
Chives
Lemon wedges

Mix together the flour and salt, make a well in the centre, pour egg whites into the well, plus half the milk, and beat thoroughly. When batter is smooth pour in rest of milk, beat well then let stand for a good 30 minutes. Heat a heavy-based non-stick fry pan, spoon in a little of the batter until it covers base of pan. Over a high heat, cook until pancake bubbles then turn and cook other side. On a warmed plate, stack the pancakes and place in a low oven until all are cooked. Serve either as illustrated (see p.77) or take a slice of smoked salmon, squeeze a little lemon juice on top and roll in a pancake. Put a dollop of yoghurt on top, sprinkle on some chopped chives and serve with lemon wedges.

SAVOURY SPRING SAUSAGES with FETA CHEESE and APPLE PURÉE

This will put a spring in your sausages, Missus! Serve it up while quoting the old Greek saying, 'Every day and in every way, you get Feta and Feta and Feta.' (Oh well, please yourselves!)

100 g (4 oz) fresh wholemeal bread crumbs
100 g (4oz) crumbled feta cheese
½ small leek, washed and very finely chopped
2 spring onions, finely chopped
½ tsp English mustard powder
15 g (1 tbsp) chopped parsley
4 egg whites
Semi-skimmed milk
Flour
15-45 ml (2-3 tbsp) vegetable oil

For the purée:

450 g (1 lb) cooking apples
30 ml (2 tbsp) honey or equivalent sweetener

In a good sized bowl mix together the bread crumbs, cheese, leeks, spring onions, mustard and parsley. Season to taste. Add the egg whites and use a fork to blend the mixture until it binds. If the mixture is too dry, add a little milk. Divide mixture into 8 portions, shape into sausages and roll in flour. Heat the oil in a non-stick pan and fry the sausages for 5-6 minutes, turning them all the time, until golden brown. Delicious hot or cold. For the purée, simply peel and core the apples, cut them into small pieces and, in a heavy saucepan, cook them gently in 3-4 tbsp water until soft. Add the honey and cook until thick. Drain off excess liquid. Use a potato masher to remove any lumps.

- SIDE DISHES -

(3-4 servings)

TOMATOES, ONIONS and MUSHROOMS on WHOLEMEAL TOAST

This tasty toasty is bliss – a blend of Mum's methods and Tel's Oz approach.

- Olive oil
- 1 large Spanish onion, cut into thickish slices (or rings)
- 1-2 beef tomatoes, roughly chopped
- 110 g (4 oz) dark mushrooms, roughly chopped
- Tabasco
- Worcestershire Sauce

In a little olive oil, fry the onions until soft and just turning brown at the edges. Stir in the tomatoes; cook for a further 2-3 minutes, then add the mushrooms and cook for a further 2-3 minutes. Sprinkle over a little Tabasco and Worcestershire sauce, stir well, then spoon immediately over hot wholemeal toast on individual plates.

CORN FRITTERS

A deep South 'Wheat Star Named Desire'

2 cups of corn kernels (tinned or cooked from frozen)
3 egg whites
5 ml (1 tsp) vegetable oil
75 ml (3 fl oz) semi-skimmed milk
10 g (2 tsp) baking powder
100 g (4 oz) rye flour

You may either purée all the ingredients in a food processor, or mix all the ingredients except for the corn and add the whole kernels at the last minute before frying – the way I prefer it. Heap tablespoons of the mixture into a lightly greased (with vegetable oil) non-stick pan and cook until golden, turning once.

MUESLI LOAF

100 g (4 oz) muesli
15 g (1 tbsp) brown sugar
100 g (4 oz) chopped, stoned dates
50 g (2 oz) chopped, mixed nuts
275 ml (½ pint) semi-skimmed milk
100 g (4 oz) wheatmeal self-raising flour

In a bowl, soak muesli, sugar, dates and nuts in the milk for approximately 30 minutes. Mix in flour gently and turn into greased 900g (2lb) loaf tin. Bake in a pre-heated oven (180C/350F/gas mark 4) for about an hour.

AUBERGINE STUFFED MUSHROOMS

There's a hint of Hellenic here – aubergine is one of the great Greek vegetables.

1 good-sized aubergine (egg plant)
2 garlic cloves (crushed)
Juice of 1 lime
50 g (2 oz) wholemeal breadcrumbs
25 ml (1 tbsp) tomato purée
Fresh basil
8 large open-cap mushrooms
25 g (10 oz) Edam cheese (grated)
60 ml (4 tbsp) vegetable consommé

Pre-heat oven to 220C/425F/gas mark 7. Cut aubergine lengthways and place skin side uppermost in a baking dish. Cook in oven for about 25-30 minutes until soft. When cool, scoop out flesh and put into food processor with the garlic, lime juice, bread crumbs, tomato purée and a few sprigs of basil. Blend for 10-15 seconds. Have mushrooms ready in the baking dish, spoon mixture into them, sprinkle grated Edam on top, gently pour the consommé around the mushrooms, cover and cook for about 20 minutes. Remove cover and cook for a further 5 minutes. With a draining spoon place onto serving dish and garnish with a little more fresh chopped basil before serving.

ROAST BANANAS in WALNUT OIL

How to make one of the richest-in-fibre fruits taste even more delicious.

8 small bananas, peeled
30 g (2 tbsp) honey
Finely chopped nuts
Walnut oil

Heat oven to 180C/350F/gas mark 4. Brush bananas with the honey, roll them in the finely chopped nuts, and arrange in a non-stick baking dish. Roast for about 15-20 minutes in the oven, turning once. Serve on a platter with any excess honey poured over them.

FRENCH TOAST with HONEY

Don't let me hold you up. This is too good not to rush into. Go! go! go! Clouzot.

3-4 egg whites
3-4 slices wholemeal bread
Nutmeg
Low-fat spread
Honey

Whisk the egg whites in a bowl, then soak wholemeal bread slices (crusts on) in the mixture until absorbed (a couple of minutes). Heat a little low-fat spread in a non-stick pan. Cook the bread slices as you would an omelette, turning once. Both sides should be golden brown and feather-light in texture. Turn out onto plate and pour honey generously over the French toast. Sprinkle nutmeg on top. And for an extra treat, top it off with slivers of your favourite fruit, such as plums, apricots, nectarines or peaches.

'Shaping up is not so hard to do
But it can be the making of you
You better believe it'

From 'Do it!'
K. Clayton

Jazz Salad Niçoise

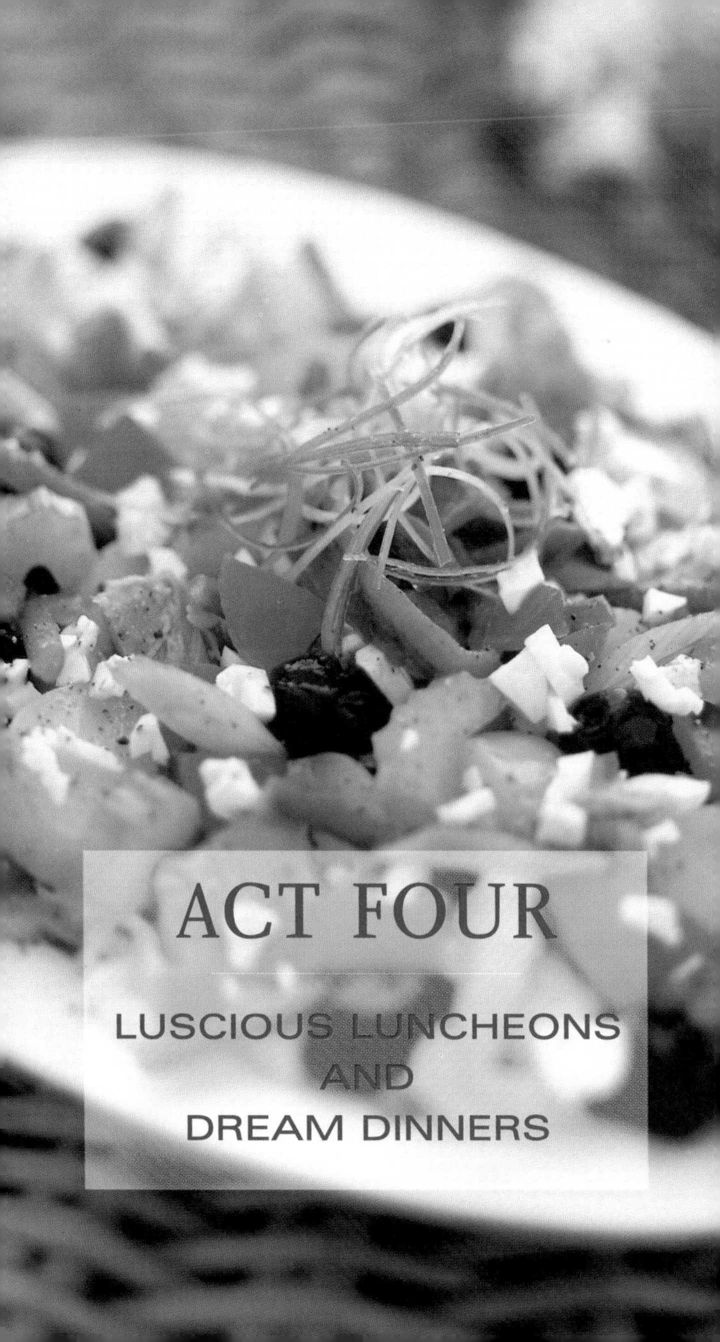

ACT FOUR

LUSCIOUS LUNCHEONS AND DREAM DINNERS

Formality without necessarily being FORMAL. That's my aim for luncheons and dinners (not *lunch* and *supper,* by the way). My mum was famous for her spectacular, cleverly cooked Sunday roasts. A side of beef the size of Bristol, sizzling like a bonfire, arrived on the table to be apportioned by my father, who could carve slices like a master chef. Us kids sat impatiently slavering. A vast Yorkshire pudding pulsed and simmered on the plate, succulent with juices from the meat (not nimpy-pimpy hydrated little singles). Gleaming roast potatoes that said crisply, 'Eat me!' and fresh greens by the barrel load. If we'd been wearing different clothes it could have been a scene from *Pickwick.* I carry all this in my memory of tastes and kitchen smells, and now I must depart from these memories in these recipes! Discipline! discipline!

In my case luncheons traditionally take place on a Sunday, which comes from doing eight shows a week over the years and having just one day off (don't talk to actors about politicians' hours!) Everyone in show business knows that *Sunday-sweet-Sunday* feeling very well, and we start to dream about it from Monday onwards. (Then your agent rings with a Sunday concert and you're F–izzically up for it, *of course!*).

When I'm not working, I try to arrange my entertaining for mid-week, especially in the summer. Saturdays, friends and family stay over and roll out of bed expecting Sunday breakfast and find they get the

Fizzical workout first (you should hear the terms of endearment!).

I think luncheons should be bright affairs decorated with wild flowers, a table of colourful pottery and ceramics, eye-catching serving platters and plates. Vibrant napkins will do the trick and there are some wonderful modern designs around. Seek and ye shall find. Setting the scene: seat guests at a table decked with a glorious mixed salad and a tempting basket of healthy breads, then present a banquet platter with a vast ring of steaming rice or pasta, surrounding a centrepiece of piping hot chicken made with red wine, leeks and ginger. Demand nothing less than a standing ovation. Next comes the raising of wine glasses and your first sip warms, rewards and reminds. It is, and should be, a special moment.

Dinner and dinner parties are times when subtlety and sophistication are expected and I think that's why they are more complex. Why do we have *dinners*? *The Dictionary of Manners* defines them as 'formal, social occasions'. I half expect them to add, 'First, brief your butler'. To deal with the occasion, butler or no, make yourself a checklist. Here's mine:

1. Who's coming, at what time and what to wear. This is a woman's prime concern and invariably becomes the man's when we say, 'You're not going out in *that*!'

2. Decide menu – and for nibbles, see Act Two: Patés, Dips and Spreads.

3. When to shop?

4. Atmosphere. Lighting (I love candlelight, subtle colours, soft music).

5. Style and theme for laying the table (do it early) and seating plan.

6. Get your man to uncork the wine at least one hour ahead.

7. Time the courses to allow for intercourse conversation.

8. Find out if husband is telling that joke about the Australian cricket fans and the two melons – *again*!

There are question marks over dinner planning that never seem to arise with luncheons. I tip my hat to the socialites who keep a book recording who came to dinner and when, what dishes were served, and grade the success of each evening by scoring it out of ten.

Atmosphere – bring out the chunky wine goblets and the best family linen, not because you want to impress but because they conjure up memories and increase your enjoyment of the occasion. Remember, dinner is one fitness food event that you need time to plan and prepare. Why? Because *you* need to enjoy it too.

Another opening – another show!

- STARTERS -

(All recipes 3-4 servings)

COLD CREAM of BRUSSELS SPROUTS SOUP with PINE NUTS

Some people tend to eat Brussels sprouts only at Christmas and don't realise that, puréed in a cold soup, they take on a whole new taste sensation and can be enjoyed all year round.

1 medium onion, finely sliced
vegetable oil
900 g (2lbs) Brussels sprouts (frozen
if out of season)
570 ml (1 pt) semi-skimmed milk
15 g (1 tbsp) pine nuts
30 ml (2 tbsp) Greek yoghurt or fromage frais
Chopped chives
Freshly ground black pepper

Sauté onion in a saucepan with a little vegetable oil. Add sprouts and milk and bring to the boil. Reduce heat, simmer for 10-15 minutes or until sprouts have softened. Purée in a blender or through a sieve. Allow to cool, place in fridge until ready to serve. Pour into bowls, add a dollop of yoghurt, scatter pine nuts on top and finish off with chopped chives and black pepper.

CHILLED HONEY and MINT SOUP

Terry is a honey freak. Having put this recipe to the Tel-Test, I can safely recommend it to you. The blending of honey and mint is really zingy and uplifting, whetting the appetite for what's to follow.

Corn oil
4 shallots, finely chopped
1 Ogen or Honeydew melon, peeled and chopped into small chunks
570 ml (1 pt) vegetable stock (see p. 25)
15 ml (1 tbsp) white wine vinegar
3-4 good sprigs fresh mint
150 ml (¼ pt) low-fat natural yoghurt
60 ml (4 tbsp) honey

In a solid-based pan, sauté the shallots in a little corn oil for about 5 minutes. Add the melon and cook for a further 5 minutes. Add stock, bring to boil and simmer for another 5 minutes. Allow to cool, then add vinegar, chopped mint leaves from 2 sprigs, the yoghurt and honey, mixing with a wooden spoon all the time. You can blend for 10-15 seconds if you wish. Chill and serve in individual bowls using the remaining chopped mint leaves as a garnish.

GAZPACHO

A real spring and summer favourite, this traditional Spanish soup conjures up the Costa del Sol, doesn't Costa Lot and never fails to satisfy. Served with whole-meal toast, it can be a meal in itself.

2 firm beef tomatoes – or 1 425g (14oz) can of chopped tomatoes
1 red pepper, seeded and chopped coarsely
½ small cucumber, peeled and chopped
½ medium onion, chopped
1 clove garlic, crushed
30 ml (2 tbsp) olive oil
15 ml (1 tbsp) tomato purée
15 ml (1 tbsp) white wine vinegar
Juice of 1 lemon or lime
15 g (1 tbsp) fresh basil or coriander
Whole meal croutons
Freshly ground black pepper

For the garnish:

15 g (1 tbsp) chopped red pepper
15 g (1 tbsp) chopped cucumber
15 g (1 tbsp) chopped spring onion
15 g (1 tbsp) chopped fresh parsley
1 hard-boiled egg, chopped (yolk removed)

FIZZTIP: If using whole tomatoes, place in a bowl,

pour boiling water over them and leave for about 30 seconds. Remove and gently make an incision in the skins with a sharp knife and peel off skins with your fingers. Then, for about 20 seconds, blend (in a food processor or blender) the tomatoes, pepper, cucumber, onion and garlic. Switch off. Add olive oil, purée, vinegar, lemon or lime juice, herbs and black pepper. Blend for a further 10 seconds. If final mixture is too thick, add a little cold water or tomato juice. To make garnish, combine all ingredients with a fork – don't overdo it and make them too mushy – place in a serving bowl and, along with croutons made of wholemeal bread fried in olive oil - spoon on to soup before eating.

ASPARAGUS and CHICKEN MOUSSE

Prepare for gasps from your guests. Putting asparagus and chicken together is inspired (I cannot take credit for it – this recipe is rooted in French folklore I'm told, and was once called Coq-au-Gus which sounds so absurd it must be true). Anyway, it's pretty and pretty good too!

1 400g (14 oz) can of asparagus
2 cooked chicken breasts, thinly chopped
150 ml (¼ pt) chicken stock (see p. 23)
25 g (1oz) rye flour
25 g (1oz) margarine

15 g (½ oz) gelatine
45 ml (3 tbsp) dry white wine
300 ml (½ pt) Greek yoghurt

Drain – but keep – the liquid from the can of asparagus. Chop asparagus roughly and add chopped chicken breast. Melt margarine in a pan, stir in flour and cook for 1 minute. Stir in the stock plus the liquid from the strained asparagus, bring to boil and simmer for a couple of minutes, stirring all the time; remove from heat. Fold asparagus and chicken into sauce. Separately, dissolve gelatine in the wine over a low heat, stir into the asparagus and chicken mixture and fold in the yoghurt. Put mixture into a mould tin – about 18cm (7") round and chill in the fridge. Serve with lime wedges.

OKRA SALAD

Okra is one of the great unsung vegetables. It has its own unique taste (Indians wisely use it in many of their classic dishes) and served in a salad, it's truly superb.

225 g (½ lb) fresh okra, washed carefully
1 small onion, finely chopped
2 Italian plum tomatoes, skinned, seeded and chopped
½ green pepper, seeded and finely chopped
15 ml (1 tbsp) olive oil
Oil and balsamic vinegar (for dressing)

15 g (1 tbsp) mixed chopped parsley and basil
Tabasco sauce

Slice okra about 5mm (¼") thick and cook in a little boiling water until tender. Drain. Gently sauté onion and green pepper in olive oil until tender; add tomatoes and continue cooking for a further 5-6 minutes. Combine okra, onion, tomatoes and pepper in a bowl, dress with oil and balsamic vinegar to taste, add a few drops of Tabasco, and toss gently. Keep in the fridge until ready to serve. Sprinkle generously with the parsley and basil mixture.

JAZZ SALAD NIÇOISE

A funky, chunky, scat singer's salad (in tuna with the times-a).

1 Cos or Romaine lettuce, washed and dried
10-12 spinach leaves, washed and dried
1 celery stalk, washed and roughly chopped
4 tomatoes, washed and roughly chopped
1 green pepper, seeded and roughly chopped
110 g (4 oz) cooked new potatoes
½ small cucumber, cut into chunks
110 g (4 oz) cooked French beans
15 g (1 tbsp) chopped onion or spring onion

1 200 g (7 oz) can tuna fish, drained and flaked
1 50 g (2 oz) can anchovies (in oil – not brine), drained
2 hard boiled eggs (with yolks removed), roughly chopped
50 g (2 oz) black olives
Oil and white wine vinegar for dressing
Chopped parsley

With your fingers break the lettuce and, along with the spinach leaves, lay it in a large salad bowl. Put all ingredients – except tuna, anchovies, eggs and olives – into the bowl and gently toss. Then make a well in the salad, sink in the tuna and spread four anchovies in a cross on top. Decorate with egg and olives, pour over the dressing and finish off with a sprinkling of chopped parsley.

SHIRLEY VALENTINE GREEK SALAD

Tangy, sharp and full of freshness – a salad with a bit of Greek on the side!

225 g (8 oz) Feta cheese, chopped into small chunks
4 ripe tomatoes, cut into eighths
1 small onion, cut into thin rings then halved
½ medium cucumber (peeled, cut lengthways into quarters then across into small cubes)
50 g (2 oz) black olives
Olive oil
Freshly ground black pepper
Juice of two limes

Place all ingredients into a mixing bowl (except oil, black pepper and lime juice). Toss gently just prior to serving, pour oil over salad, then the lime juice – finally add the black pepper and serve.

- MAIN COURSES -

CHICKEN CASSEROLE with RED WINE, GINGER and LEEKS

The lovely thing about a casserole is that you can cook it hours before and this makes it taste even better. Fizz-tip: An alternative serving suggestion is to drain off liquid into a jug and present the chicken and vegetables surrounded by an impressive ring of rice or pasta. A little of the liquid may be poured over the dish and the rest handed around in the jug for guests to help themselves.

1 large onion, peeled and sliced
2 leeks, washed and sliced into rings
450 g (1 lb) boneless chicken pieces
15 g (1 tbsp) finely grated ginger
5 ml (1 tsp) chopped oregano
200 g (7 oz) canned chopped tomatoes
275 ml (½ pt) red wine
Vegetable oil

Pre-heat oven to 180C/450F/gas mark 4. In a large non-stick pan with a little vegetable oil, gently brown onion and leeks for about 5 minutes; add chicken pieces, grated ginger and oregano, and cook for a further 8-10 minutes over a medium heat. In a lidded casserole, place all the ingredients, pour over the chopped tomatoes and red wine and bake for approximately 30 minutes. Perfect served with plain boiled rice – brown rice is even better.

SWEET and SOUR CHICKEN with WHOLE-WHEAT PASTA

Most of us enjoy Chinese food with rice. Here is a new Fizz-twist combining a traditional Far Eastern dish with Italian pasta. The Orient meets the amore-ent. It works.

15 ml (1 tbsp) vegetable oil
1 large onion, finely chopped
2 celery sticks, finely sliced
3-4 boneless chicken breasts, skinned
 and cut into thin slivers
10 g (2 tsp) grated ginger
30 ml (2 tbsp) honey or equivalent sweetener
10 ml (2 tsp) soy sauce
30 g (2 tbsp) chopped pineapple
15 g (1 tbsp) corn flour
30 ml (2 tbsp) white wine vinegar
275 ml (½ pt) of dry white wine

Put the vegetable oil into a wok and gently fry the chopped onion and sliced celery for about 5 minutes; then add the chicken slivers, cooking and stirring for a further 6-8 minutes until golden. Set aside on a plate. Using the same wok, add ginger, honey, soy sauce and chopped pineapple. Whilst this is simmering for a few minutes, put corn flour into a small jug, gently stir in vinegar and when blended, add the wine. Return chicken to wok and slowly pour on the liquid from the jug. Stir until the sauce thickens then simmer for a further 5 minutes. Remove from heat. Following the maker's instructions, in a pan cook enough whole-wheat pasta for 3-4 people, drain and pour sweet and sour mixture over top and gently mix in with a wooden spoon. Serve immediately.

FRESH SALMON SALAD with SAFFRON and COCONUT WILD RICE

Interestingly, wild rice – which comes from America – is not strictly a grain at all. It's a type of grass seed but it has a lovely black colour and nutty texture. The mixture of salmon, saffron and coconut gives this dish a great look as well as taste.

4 good sized salmon steaks, about 2.5cm (1") thick
small cucumber, grated
30 g (2 tbsp) chopped dill
4 spring onions, finely chopped
60 ml (4 tbsp) dry white wine
60 ml (4 tbsp) Greek yoghurt
A few strands of saffron

275 g (10 oz) wild rice
570 ml (1 pt) water
15 g (1 tbsp) desiccated coconut
Ground pepper, cayenne pepper and
paprika, to taste

Grill the salmon steaks for about 10-12 minutes, turning once, until they begin to darken slightly. Put to one side and allow to cool completely. In a bowl, put cucumber, chopped dill and spring onions; then add wine and finally, fold in yoghurt.

To cook the rice, use a wide saucepan or frying pan with a lid. Some people like to rinse rice but it isn't necessary. Put rice into pan, pour on water, bring slowly to the boil, simmer gently for about 15 minutes, then add saffron strands. Simmer for a further 10-15 minutes (wild rice takes longer to cook than conventional rice). Don't stir. The rice is cooked when the water is completely absorbed. Sieve into a bowl, let cool and, before serving, fluff with a fork adding the coconut and a little ground pepper.

Serve salmon on a bed of wild rice, spooning yoghurt mixture on top. Sprinkle with a little cayenne pepper or paprika before serving.

ROAST PORK with BROCCOLI and WATER CHESTNUTS

This is an unusual dish in that the pork is roasted in apple juice – and it does work. Served on a platter surrounded with small minted new potatoes, it's a great Sunday luncheon dish.

4 large or 8 small lean pork steaks
450 g (1 lb) broccoli florets
1 large cooking apple, peeled and sliced
400 g (14 oz) can of water chestnuts, drained
275 ml (½ pt) cloudy apple juice
Chopped parsley for garnish

Pre-heat oven to 180C/350F/gas mark 4. Lay the pork steaks in a casserole dish, pour on the apple juice, put lid on top and place in oven for about 20 minutes. Whilst pork is cooking, place broccoli and apple into a pan of boiling water and simmer for about 5 minutes, then drain. Remove casserole from oven, spoon the broccoli and apple on top and add the water chestnuts. Spoon apple juice over the casserole and return to oven for a further 20-25 minutes. Sprinkle parsley on top before serving.

APPLE, CABBAGE and POTATO CASSEROLE

You don't need to be a vegetarian to enjoy this hearty autumn and winter dish; you'll probably be surprised at how many second helpings will be called for.

2 cooking apples, peeled, cored and thinly sliced
1 small cabbage – any variety – thinly sliced
2 baking potatoes, peeled and thinly sliced
Low-fat spread
30 g (2 tbsp) whole wheat breadcrumbs
275 ml (½ pt) low-fat natural yoghurt
30-45 g (2-3 tbsp) Gouda cheese, grated

Pre-heat oven to 180C/350F/gas mark 4. Arrange one-third of the apple, cabbage and potatoes in a layer in a casserole; dot with low fat spread. Following same procedure, continue with a second layer and a third, piling the contents high in the centre (don't worry, it'll cook down). Pour over the yoghurt and bake for about 30 minutes. Then, remove from oven, sprinkle with bread crumbs and grated cheese, and carry on cooking for a further 8-10 minutes or until the top browns and forms a crust.

BAKED OYSTERS with TOMATO BROWN RICE RISOTTO

Oysters have a naturally high oil content and paired with brown rice – the rice with the highest fibre, vitamin and mineral content because it's the natural grain – this is a thrilling new way of enjoying both.

275 g (10 oz) long grain brown rice
275 ml (10 fl oz) fish stock (see p. 24)
275 ml (1/2 pt) water
1 medium onion, finely chopped
30 g (2 tbsp) chopped sun-dried tomatoes
15 g (1 tbsp) minced tarragon
30 g (2 tbsp) low fat spread
12-16 large oysters in half-shells
3 spring onions, finely chopped
60 ml (4 tbsp) dry white wine (or dry sherry)
5 g (1 tsp) of minced parsley
2 cloves of garlic, very finely chopped
(not crushed)
30-45 ml (2-3 tbsp) whole meal bread crumbs
Grated Edam or Gouda cheese

We start with the risotto. Melt low-fat spread in a heavy saucepan and sauté onion for about 4-5 minutes. Stir in uncooked rice and cook for a further 4-5 minutes until all grains are coated with spread. Add fish stock and gently bring to the boil. Turn down to simmer and slowly add the water, as required. Cooking time varies but it usually takes about 18-20 minutes for the stock to be absorbed. If rice requires more liquid, add further water but don't overcook.

In between keeping an eye on the risotto, pre-heat oven to 180C/350F/gas mark 4. Place oysters on a foil-covered baking dish to retain liquid. In a small pan, heat the spring onions with the wine until most of it has evaporated. Combine onions with the parsley, garlic, bread crumbs and low-fat spread to make a paste. Scoop a little of this paste on to each oyster, sprinkle with the grated cheese and bake for about 10 minutes until the cheese has melted. The rice should now be ready. Before serving, fluff with a fork, adding chopped sun-dried tomatoes and tarragon. Make a ring of rice on each plate and sit the oysters in the middle.

MONKFISH and KING PRAWN KEBABS

Outdoors or indoors, this is a popular kebab combination and doubly delicious served with simple and fluffy plain boiled rice.

Spinach
Purple Sprouting
Toasted, slivered almonds
450 g (1lb) monkfish steaks cut into
bite-sized cubes
Cherry tomatoes
12-18 king prawns, shelled
Green pepper, cut into squares
Shallots, peeled
Vegetable oil
Lemon wedges

Firstly, in a pan cook the spinach and purple sprouting until tender. Drain and put into an oven-proof dish, sprinkling the vegetables with toasted slivered almonds. Put into a warm oven. Next, on kebab skewers, alternate the pieces of monkfish with the tomatoes, prawns, peppers and shallots, repeating until skewers are full. Brush on a little oil and grill until fish has turned golden and begins to brown, turning a couple of times. When cooked, place the kebabs on a bed of the greens; garnish with lemon wedges.

- DESSERTS -

Here you will find desserts rich in fruit, designed to complement the previous starters and/or main courses. You can mix and match from this selection. The harvesting of fruits and combinations of their colours when gathered together, has always excited me. Included in this collection, at the request of frequent guests of gargantuan appetite, is my own version of home-baked apple pie.

SUMMER FRUIT COMPOTE

1 cup of dry white wine
30 ml (1 tbsp) honey or equivalent sweetener
3 whole cloves
½ tsp ground ginger
1 cinnamon stick
2 large pears, peeled and cut into
  uniformed pieces
4 peaches, halved and pitted
6 plums, halved and pitted
Melon balls (made from half an Ogen
  or similar melon)
Sprig of mint

In a small pan, simmer together wine, honey, cloves,

ginger and cinnamon for about 10 minutes. Add pears and peaches and poach until tender – approximately 15 minutes. Cool and put in the fridge. Before serving, remove spices, add plums and melon balls, stir gently and garnish with mint leaves.

FRESH PINEAPPLE with SHERRY and MINT

1 large, fresh pineapple (or 2 small ones)
Dry sherry
Honey
Shredded mint leaves

It's essential the pineapple is ripe, so test by pressing the centre-bottom, which should be soft and orange coloured. Cut pineapple lengthways; cut out fruit in neat wedges using a sharp knife, thus leaving a shell. Discard core, slice pineapple into bite-sized chunks, combine with a mixture of sherry and honey to taste and spoon back into shells. Sprinkle with mint.

HARVEYS SHERRY JELLY with MIXED FRUITS

15 g (1 tbsp) gelatine
150 ml (¼ pint) of hot water
15 ml (1 tbsp) honey
15 ml (1 tbsp) lemon juice
30 ml (2 tbsp) orange juice
30 ml (2 tbsp) Harveys Bristol Cream sherry
1 large fresh peach, peeled and sliced
1 large fresh nectarine, peeled and sliced
6-8 green seedless grapes, washed
and halved
45 ml (3 tbsp) low-fat natural yoghurt

In a heat-proof glass bowl, dissolve gelatine by sprinkling it over the hot (but not boiling) water. Add honey, lemon and orange juice and sherry. Place in fridge until gelatine cools and begins to set. Then, stir in the peach, nectarine and grapes and fold in the yoghurt. Chill thoroughly until firm. Alternatively, you can transfer jelly mixture to a mould, which has been rinsed out with cold water, and when set turn out on to a serving plate.

ORANGES IN RED WINE

30 ml (2 tbsp) honey
30 ml (2 tbsp) red wine
1 cinnamon stick
3-4 cloves
2-3 lemon slices
2 large navel oranges, peeled, pithed and cut into slices

Combine honey, red wine, cinnamon stick, cloves and lemon slices in a saucepan, bring to the boil, and simmer for about 5-10 minutes. Put oranges into a serving dish and, through a sieve, pour the hot liquid over them and refrigerate until ready to serve.

FRESH STRAWBERRY ICE

2 small punnets of fresh strawberries, washed and hulled
A little honey (or equivalent sweetener)
30 ml (2 tbsp) water
Juice of ½ an orange
Juice of ½ a lime
15 ml (1 tbsp) white rum (optional)

Purée all ingredients in a blender. Chill in the freezer until the mixture begins to solidify (timing depends on individual freezers but certainly check after 20 minutes), remove and whisk, and return to the freezer. Take out about 20 minutes before required and serve in stemmed glasses with a fresh strawberry on top of each.

BANANAS with YOGHURT, HONEY and CHOPPED NUTS

4 bananas, peeled and sliced
Lemon juice
60 ml (4 tbsp) Greek yoghurt
15 ml (1 tbsp) Greek honey
Chopped nuts
Fresh mint

Slice bananas lengthways, place on four serving plates and sprinkle with lemon juice to prevent discolouring. Dollop a tablespoon of yoghurt onto each banana; drip a teaspoon of honey on top and finally garnish with chopped nuts and fresh mint. Serve immediately.

ANITA'S AMOROUS APPLE PIE

So named because, and I say this with an absolute absence of modesty, everyone loves it – YES!!! I almost always have to make two! My mum taught me how to make pastry so you might say she has a finger in this pie.

4 or 6 Bramley apples (I like ample apple)
1 cinnamon stick
2.5 cm (1") piece of fresh ginger, peeled
8 cloves in a little muslin bag
50-75 g (2-3 oz) sugar or equivalent
  sweetener or 30 ml (2 tbsp) honey
Lemon or lime juice
Grated zest of lemon or lime

In large saucepan cover all ingredients with water and poach until tender. Drain and cool. Remove cinnamon, ginger and cloves.

FIZZTIP: Don't throw away juice – use it to make sauce or jelly.

For the pastry:

225 g (8 oz) flour (self-raising or whole meal)
Pinch of salt
50 g (2 oz) vegetable lard, e.g. Cookeen
Cool water to bind

50 g (2 oz) low-fat spread

Sift the flour with the salt into a large bowl. Cut the lard into small pieces and add to the flour. With cool washed hands, rub the lard into the flour working lightly with your fingers and lifting a little to let in air. When the mixture looks like bread crumbs, add cool water a little at a time and, with a palette knife, mix into the dough. Spread the low-fat spread over a large Pyrex plate, roll out half the dough to cover base of plate and trim surplus cleanly around the edge. (Optional choice: cover the bottom layer of dough with apricot jam).

Spoon the cooled apple mixture over the base and cover with the other half of the rolled dough. Pinch or use a fork to crimp the edges. Pierce the top 4 times with a fork. For a glazed top, brush with low-fat milk and sprinkle on a little caster sugar. Bake in a moderate oven (180-200C/350-400F/gas mark 4-6) for approximately 40 minutes, until golden. Serve with low-fat yoghurt or low-fat ice cream.

'I'm pushin' and pullin', runnin and ridin'
Skippin' and sweatin', slippin' and slidin'
I'm bumpin' and jumpin' and it's sumpin'
When I'm pumpin' iron!

I'm a vulture for physical culture
Not to mention dynamic tension
You know you really could do worse
than be a mister universe'

From 'Pumpin Iron!'
K. Clayton

Prawn and Brown Rice Pilaf

ACT FIVE

LET'S PARTY

Fizzical Fun Food. Parties ... Celebrations ... Anniversaries ... Birthdays! ... And the you-don't-need-an-excuse-for-one ... party!

Once again it's pre-prep, pre-prep, pre-prep. Buffet food is the way to go because it can be prepared well in advance. I've found that the secret of success for party givers and guests is not to try for too many dishes. Less is more. Concentrate on three or four impressive, abundant main dishes which will cater for a full evening of browsing eaters. At least one dish should be guest-gaspworthy – in short, your showpiece (actually a show-off piece). Example: succulent whole Scottish salmon* with parsley sauce and lime wedges, accompanied by a tureen piled high with minted new potatoes shoulder to pod with a profusion of petit pois. A generous glass bowl of Gazpacho salad and a picnic basket of mixed whole meal breads and Melba toast. Use an ice cream scoop to pile a large shallow dish with snooker-size balls of butter-substitute.

As, with the exception of the Fatburner section, we are virtually abstaining from red meat because of its fat and cholesterol content, there are no meat recipes in this section. However, if you feel you need an occasional red meat treat, choose lean beef or lamb and cook it the day before, leave it to cool so that any fat can be skimmed off the top. Many of my friends in show business invariably arrive after a show, sometimes well past midnight. When I know this is going to happen, I make an all-nighter Thespians Hot Pot with chicken or turkey (see p. 143).

***FIZZTIP:** For the salmon, slice narrow ends from cucumbers, finely slice a collection of small circles, halve them and lay carefully along your salmon until you have covered your fish in green 'scales'. This decoration has two purposes: it rates high on the gaspometer and keeps the salmon beautifully moist. A whole cartwheel of low-fat Brie and a full round of Edam cheese looks (and is) plentiful, always goes down well, and eases the conscience of guests who are shy of significant portions. (Actually, come to think of it, I don't seem to have any friends who suffer from such reservations!).

If you want to bake a cake to focus the occasion, make for a happening and flag a moment, try the De-Luxe Celebration Fruit Cake (see p.150). It is a seriously great party cake, rich in fruity nutrient (with a little clandestine cognac).

Remember, you're feeding the five thousand with Fizzical Food, not fattening them up with flatulent fillings. Don't plump for the standard fare of crisps, nuts and prawn crackers (tempting though they are). Instead, try fresh crudités with a sweet and sour dip, and hors d'oeuvres of home-made whole meal pastry cups (see p. 145), filled with avocado, lemon and spring onion or Clive and Cilla's Portuguese paté (see pp. 57).

Think about the music you will play and about the atmosphere you want to create.I like to welcome guests with cool classical music, that way my friends immediately feel Mozart and Liszt (obtuse ancient musician's joke, so called because it is usually cracked by ancient musicians). One successful sequence for me is cool classicals – hint of jazz – followed by sixties pop revival (rich with tracks that everyone moves to) and New Country music, abundant with wit and great rhythm – then Sinatra for the shade of the evening.

Think about space when organising the geography of your party. Position your bar deep in a room, away from crucial doorways (people congregate around the bar).

FIZZTIP: If you have invited somebody shy, assign them to help out where guests will always talk to them – at the bar! – and watch their shyness melt right away.

Have a look at 'Act One: Kick off with a Cocktail' for liquid refreshment. It is a good idea to 'flag' non-alcoholic drinks for designated drivers (if you're behind the wheel, 'Blue Hue' is not for you!).'Cool Mac', 'Cola Cooler', 'Caribbean Creme' and 'Coconut Amore' are all fantastic new non-alcoholic fun tastes and conversation pieces.

On the alcohol front, try 'Red Wine Cup', 'Mulled Wine and Honey', 'Champagne Blonde', 'Strawberry and Mint Champagne' and 'Blue Hue'.

- LET'S PARTY! -

(All recipes approximately 10 - 12 servings)

WHOLE SALMON with PARSLEY SAUCE and LIME WEDGES

Ask 100 chefs how to poach a salmon and you'll hear 100 different opinions. All agree, however, that this dish needs careful attention. Here's mine – version 101! The size of the salmon depends on your largesse and your guests' appetites but, as a rule of thumb, you should allow about 225-275 g (8-10 oz) fish per person; thus for 12 servings, your salmon would need to be 2.75- 3.30 kg (6-7½ lb). You'll need a large fish kettle. **FIZZTIP:** try borrowing from a friendly fishmonger – or buy one, because this is a dish you'll want to indulge in again and again!)

Whole fresh salmon (as per size above)
Vegetable stock (see p. 25)
6 bay leaves
3 lemons, sliced
Approximately 24-30 black peppercorns
15 ml (1 tbsp) low-fat margarine
6-8 spring onions, finely chopped
2 carrots, diced
10 g (2 tsp) ground ginger
A whole cucumber, with skin on, sliced finely
60 g (4 tbsp) chopped parsley

570ml (1pt) Greek yoghurt
Lime wedges for garnish
Watercress

Place salmon on the kettle tray and lower into the kettle. Season with salt and pepper. Add sufficient vegetable stock to just cover it. Add bay leaves, lemon slices and peppercorns. Put on kettle lid, place on the hob (you may need to position it across two gas jets or hot plates) and cook on low heat until bubbles appear. Don't boil or the fish may break up. Lower heat so that it *barely* simmers. Allow about 4-5 minutes per 450 g (1 lb) cooking time.

FIZZTIP: When the fish has cooked, let it cool in its own liquid before removing. That said, the fish is easier to skin if it is warm rather than cold. To skin the salmon, lay it carefully on a piece of foil, cut off the fins, slit skin along the back and peel away. Using the foil as a 'lifter', turn it over and repeat. Place salmon in fridge to chill (for about an hour), remove and gently scrape off any fatty deposits that remain. It will then be ready for dressing.

In the meantime, while the fish is cooking, heat a small non-stick pan, melt the low-fat spead, stir in the spring onions, carrots and ginger, and finally the parsley. Simmer for about 5 minutes, cool, then fold in the yoghurt. Next, carefully arrange salmon on a serving platter and lay the sliced cucumber in half-circles the entire length of the fish to create a 'scales' effect (as described on page 129). Finally, spoon or pipe the parsley sauce around the edge of the platter and garnish with lime wedges and watercress.

ENDIVE with MARINATED MUSHROOMS

Endive is probably the only salad green that can be tossed with its own dressing up to 4 hours before serving and doesn't wilt. In other words, this recipe is perfect for a party.

900 g (2 lbs) fresh bite-size whole button mushrooms
1 large onion, finely chopped
1 clove garlic, crushed
15 g (1 tbsp) chopped parsley
2 bay leaves
150 ml (5 fl oz) white wine
30 ml (2 tbsp) olive or walnut oil
15 ml (1 tbsp) lemon or lime juice
12-15 whole endives
Olive oil and balsamic vinegar for dressing

Wash the mushrooms and wipe them dry with a paper towel. Put them into a large saucepan (or wok) with the onion, garlic, parsley, bay leaves, white wine, olive or walnut oil, and lemon or lime juice and bring to the boil. Reduce heat, simmer for about 5-6 minutes or until tender, stirring occasionally. Meanwhile, cut off the base of the endives, then slit lengthways, or across in 1cm (½") slices. Coat lightly with oil and balsamic vinegar, place in a large salad bowl or serving platter, and pour the mushroom mixture on top. To garnish, sprinkle chopped parsley over the platter, followed by some ground black pepper.

AVOCADO SALAD with SCHNAPPS and LIME DRESSING

Schnapps is a name for various spirits, especially Hollands gin. It comes under the heading of 'occasional treats' as the dressing is, rather like my husband the morning after, salty and sharp!

1 Cos lettuce, finely shredded
6 ripe avocados, pitted and peeled
Freshly-squeezed juice of 3 oranges
150 ml (5 fl oz) schnapps
6-8 limes – to make 150 ml (5 fl oz) of juice
5 g (1 tsp) coarse salt
Freshly ground black pepper

Firstly, cover a flat platter with the shredded lettuce. Next, slice avocados in half lengthways. Then cut across each half in 5 mm (¼") slices. Using a knife, lift the portions of avocado on to the platter and gently lay so that they look like fallen dominoes. When all avocados are on the platter, sprinkle with the orange juice, making sure all the avocados are covered. In a jug, combine the schnapps, lime juice, salt and pepper and pour over the avocados.

GRILLED or ROASTED PEPPER SALAD

This couldn't be an easier, or prettier, dish for a party. And you can make it the night before, allowing the oil and vinegar to thoroughly marinate the peppers.

10-12 peppers (ideally, a mélange of red, green, orange and yellow)
Olive oil
Balsamic vinegar
Chopped basil

Wash, halve and seed the peppers and cut into 2.5cm (1") strips. Arrange on a grill tray or roasting pan, skin side up, brush with olive oil and cook in a moderate oven. Cooking is complete when the skins become charred and slightly blistered. Put into a serving dish, alternating the colours, pour over vinegar to taste, cover with Clingfilm and refrigerate. Before serving, sprinkle with a generous helping of chopped basil.

PRAWN and BROWN RICE PILAF

Tel says this comes from an Aussie recipe known locally as 'Don't Come the Raw Prawn With Me Pilaf' which means nought to moi but apparently has some significance Down Under.

1 litre (1¾ pts) fish stock (see p. 24)
425 ml (¾ pt) dry white wine
225 g (8 oz) low-fat spread
1 large Spanish onion, chopped
450 g (1 lb) brown rice
900 g (2 lbs) prawns, fresh or
thawed from frozen
Juice of 1 lemon
30 g (2 tbsp) parsley, chopped
4-5 spring onions or shallots, finely chopped
Ground black pepper

Combine fish stock and white wine in a jug. Melt low-fat spread in a large saucepan and cook onion until soft. Add uncooked rice and fry gently until it takes on an opaque appearance; slowly pour in the stock and wine, stirring all the while. Bring to the boil then turn down heat to simmer for about 30-35 minutes (remember, brown rice takes longer to cook than white). Should more liquid be required, add water. When the rice is tender and the liquid absorbed, gently blend in the prawns and the lemon juice. Season to taste. Put rice on to a warmed serving platter, sprinkle with parsley, spring onions or shallots, and ground black pepper.

FENNEL, CUCUMBER and RADISH SALAD

Colourful crunch and come back for more.

2 medium cucumbers
3-4 fennel bulbs
10-12 radishes
30 g (2 tbsp) finely chopped chives
30 g (2 tbsp) finely chopped mint
2 garlic cloves, crushed
Olive oil
White wine vinegar

Peel the cucumbers and slice into 5 mm (¼") segments, remove the feathery tops from the fennel and cut into 5 mm (¼") segments and slice the radishes. Combine all in a serving dish with the chives, mint and garlic. Just before serving, splash with olive oil and vinegar, and top off with freshly ground black pepper.

TUNA PASTA with SATSUMA and PETIT POIS

A surprisingly light party dish for summer that requires the minimum of cooking – just the pasta and petit pois – and looks utterly tempting. Serve cold.

700 g (1½ lbs) whole-wheat macaroni
2 x 450 g (1 lb) tins of tuna in oil, flaked
6-8 small satsumas, peeled, pithed and sectioned
225 g (½ lb) petit pois, cooked from frozen
45 g (3 tbsp) chopped basil
Lime wedges, for garnish
Olive oil

Cook the macaroni in plenty of boiling water, drain under cold running water, and put to one side. In a large bowl, combine the flaked tuna, satsuma sections, petit pois and half the basil. Fold the mixture into the macaroni, sprinkle the remaining basil on top along with a couple of tablespoons of olive oil, and finish off with ground black pepper. Serve with lime wedges.

MARINATED CHICKEN WINGS

Don't get in a flutter – this swinging, winging clucker will simply fly off the plate.

30-45 ml (2-3 tbsp) soy sauce

150 ml (¼ pt) pineapple juice
150 ml (¼ pt) dry white wine
150 ml (¼ pt) safflower oil
2 garlic cloves, crushed
30-45 ml (2-3 tbsp) honey
5 g (1 tsp) ground ginger
24 chicken wings
Ground black pepper

In a large jug, combine the soy sauce, pineapple juice, wine, oil, garlic, honey and ginger. Pour over the chicken wings in a flame-proof casserole and marinate overnight (for at least 15 hours). Pre-heat oven to 180C/350F/gas mark 4. Place casserole in the oven for at least 1 hour, until caramelised and crisp. Serve hot or at room temperature.

CHILLED FRESH HADDOCK with ORANGE SAUCE

The firmness and flavour of haddock with the tangy taste of orange sauce.

700 g (1½ lbs) haddock fillets, skinned and cubed
3 medium oranges, peeled, pithed and sectioned
1 Spanish onion, coarsely chopped
1.35 kg (3 lbs) fresh spinach, washed

10 g (2 tsp) ground nutmeg
425 ml (¾ pt) freshly squeezed orange juice
15 g (1 level tbsp) corn flour
Chopped chives

Pre-heat oven to 180C/350F/gas mark 4. Place fish cubes in a covered flame-proof casserole and mix in the orange segments, chopped onion and a little orange juice. Cook in the oven for about 10-15 minutes. Meanwhile, cook the spinach, drain well, and chop it roughly, adding the nutmeg. Put to one side. Grate the rind from one orange. Make a paste of the corn flour with a little orange juice, add the rest of the juice and the rind. In a saucepan, bring the liquid to the boil, stirring all the time. If it's too thick, add some of the juice from the cooked fish. Remove from the heat and allow it to cool. Finally, arrange the spinach on a platter, lay the haddock and other ingredients from the casserole on top and, when cool, cover with Clingfilm and refrigerate. Before serving, stir the orange sauce and pour over the fish and spinach platter. Top off with chopped chives.

CHICKEN with LIME and ARTICHOKE HEARTS

A wholesome dish best kept warm on a hot plate so guests can return for more.

- 12 skinned chicken joints (thighs, wings and drumsticks mixed)
- 30 ml (2 tbsp) corn oil
- 1 Spanish onion, peeled and chopped
- 2 x 450 g (1 lb) tins of broad beans
- Grated rind of 2 limes and the juice of 4 limes
- 2 x 450 g (1 lb) tins of artichoke hearts, drained and halved
- 30 g (2 tbsp) chopped parsley
- 45 g (3 tbsp) toasted almond slivers

Dry-fry the chicken joints in a large non-stick pan for 5-6 minutes, until sealed and slowly turning brown all over. Add the oil and chopped onion and continue to cook on a medium-high heat for a further 5-6 minutes. Add the broad beans, lime rind and juice, and cook for a further 10-15 minutes. Then, add the artichokes and parsley and continue cooking for another 8-10 minutes. Transfer to a flameproof casserole/dish, sprinkle the toasted almond slivers on top and grill under a high flame until sizzling; serve immediately. This is equally good served at room temperature.

GAZPACHO SALAD

If you're a fan of the Spanish chilled soup (see p. 104), you'll become an addict of this equally nutritious salad.

4-5 beef tomatoes, halved and sliced
1½ large cucumbers, peeled and finely diced
4 green peppers, seeded and roughly chopped
2 red onions, cut into thin rings
6-8 spring onions, finely chopped
Olive oil
Red wine vinegar
3 garlic cloves, crushed
Chopped parsley

In a glass salad bowl, simply put a layer of tomatoes, cucumber, peppers, onion and a sprinkling of spring onions, and repeat this process until there's nothing left. In a separate jug, blend two parts oil to one part vinegar with a whisk or fork, add garlic, and just before serving, pour dressing over the salad. Sprinkle with parsley.

THESPIANS TURKEY HOT POT

This is my dish to cater for late arrivals. Thespians Hot Pot also tastes better the longer it cooks. It's an ideal party dish and great for those guests who like to take seconds and thirds as the evening draws on, shadows fall, the sun goes down, the moon comes up, and thespians are still making their entrance with the same old actors' gag: 'What's this, another turkey?!'

2.75 kg (6 lbs) turkey breasts, skinned and cut into bite-sized pieces
Olive oil
3 large Spanish onions, chopped
60 g (4 tbsp) plain flour
1.5 ml (2½ pts) hot water
Salt and pepper to taste
275 ml (½ pt) dry white wine
15-20 g (3-4 tsp) fresh sage, chopped
4-6 sprigs of fresh thyme
3-4 bay leaves
6 large carrots, peeled and diced
1.8 kg (4 lbs) potatoes, peeled and cut into chip-thickness slices
Low-fat spread

Pre-heat oven to 325F/170C/gas mark 3. Put a large frying pan on the hob, turn heat up high and brown the meat – a handful at a time – in about 4-6 tbsp olive oil.

As the meat browns, transfer it to an oven-proof casserole. Then fry the onions in the oil (you may need to add a little more oil) until browned. Next, gradually stir in the flour until it's absorbed, then begin to *slowly* pour in the hot water until mixture starts to thicken. Be sure to stir all the time or, better still, use a whisk. Season with salt and pepper and reduce the flame until mixture gently simmers. Now add the white wine and simmer for a further 5 minutes.

Now back to the casserole. Sprinkle the sage and thyme over the meat and add the bay leaves. Gently fold all the carrots and two-thirds of the potatoes into the meat then top it off with a layer of the remaining potatoes, overlapping them in circles. Add a few small knobs of low-fat spread to the top layer of potatoes. Carefully pour the hot stock over the meat and vegetables. Leaving casserole uncovered, place in the oven on the lowest shelf and cook for about 10-15 minutes. Remove, cover tightly with foil AND the casserole lid and cook for 2 hours, removing the lid for the final 30 minutes. If you like a crispy top, remove the foil and place the dish under a high grill for 3-5 minutes before serving. This dish can happily simmer away on the lowest oven setting or on a hot-plate.

WHOLE MEAL PASTRY CUPS

(for Appetisers)

A delightful change from canapés, which can be very time consuming. You can make the cups well in advance and fill them with the dips and patés of your choice! Delicious, for example, with Avocado Dip (see p. 56). The following recipe makes about 10-15 cups, depending on thickness of the pastry and the size of the patty tins* used for baking.

250 g (8 oz) whole meal flour
Pinch of salt
125 g (4 oz) low-fat spread
60 ml (4 tbsp) cold water

Combine the flour and salt in a bowl, make a well, and put in the low-fat spread. Gradually add cold water and stir with a knife until evenly blended, then shape into a ball. Wrap in Clingfilm and chill in the fridge for 30 minutes. Roll out on a floured board to about 5 mm (¼") thick. Use a 5 cm (2") pastry cutter to cut into rounds. Put rounds into the patty tin, press down to shape correctly. To bake blind, line each cup with a little foil and fill it with dried lentils or rice (to prevent pastry bubbling up during cooking). Cook in a medium oven for about 30 minutes. Leave to cool and store in air-tight container.

*Patty tins, for baking, come in various shapes and are available in 8, 10 or 12 cup sizes. Choose the one that suits you best.

POACHED PEARS

Fizz-tale: This dish originated in the French Foreign Legion and was popular with recruits who could not spell 'desert'. Some were overcome by their incapacity, ran away to restaurants in Montmartre and became desserters, with two esses.

12 *hard* pears, peeled, with stalks left on and with bottoms sliced across so they'll stand up straight
275 ml (½ pt) vermouth
90 ml (6 tbsp) honey
225 g (½ lb) blueberries
Fromage frais
Cinnamon

Place the pears upright in a large high-sided pan with the vermouth and honey. Bring slowly to the boil, cover and simmer for 10 minutes. Stir in the blueberries and cook for a further five minutes. Cool, place in a serving dish and chill. Spoon the liquid over the pears to give them a glaze and serve with low-fat natural fromage frais sprinkled with cinnamon.

PASSION FRUIT ICE CREAM

Passion fruit is considered by many to be an aphrodisiac. Don't let anyone have seconds of this. I refuse to be held responsible!

1.2 litres (2 pts) semi-skimmed milk
50 g (2 oz) custard powder
30 ml (2 tbsp) honey
6-8 passion fruit, halved with flesh and pips placed in a bowl and skins discarded

In a non-stick saucepan, using a little of the milk, blend the custard powder into a watery paste; add the milk gradually or the powder will become lumpy. Add the rest of the milk, bring to the boil, stirring continuously, and, when thick, remove from the heat. When coolish, add the honey and the flesh and pips from the passion fruit. Pour into a freezer-proof dish or bowl and freeze for about 50-60 minutes. Remove, beat – preferably in a food processor or blender – and re-freeze for at least 3 hours. Allow to thaw for 20 minutes before serving.

FOUR BERRY CREAM COMPOTE

This is an interesting dish because you can either present it as indicated (i.e. a compote of fruits), or blend the ingredients in a food processor or liquidiser and, hey presto, you have a creamy mousse! However, this will need a little longer in the fridge and may benefit from freezing for about an hour prior to serving. The last time I did this, I wished I'd doubled the quantity.

1 punnet of strawberries, washed, hulled and quartered
1 punnet of blackberries, washed
1 punnet of blueberries, washed
1 punnet of raspberries, washed
1 litre (1¾ pts) Greek yoghurt
15 ml (1 tbsp) honey (or equivalent sweetener to taste)
Mint sprigs for garnish

Combine all fruits, yoghurt and honey together and chill for at least 45 minutes before serving. Garnish with mint sprigs.

PEACH and BANANA MOUSSE

Another joyous and colour-enhanced blend of two favourite fruits to grace any party desserts buffet.

45 g (3 tbsp) powdered gelatine
150 ml (¼ pt) hot (but not boiling) water
8 medium peaches
4 large bananas
425 ml (¾ pt) Greek yoghurt
30 ml (2 tbsp) honey (or equivalent sweetener)
6 egg whites blended with 150 ml (¼ pt) water
Mixed peel to decorate

Sprinkle the gelatine on to hot water and stir well until completely dissolved. Set aside for 15 minutes. Place peaches in a large bowl, pour boiling water over them and, after a minute or so, drain, skin, remove stones and slice them. Blend the peaches, peeled bananas and yoghurt in a blender or food processor then transfer to a large mixing bowl and stir in the cooled gelatine. Whisk the egg whites until they form a peak and fold them, gently but thoroughly, through the purée. Refrigerate in individual glasses or in the bowl for at least 2 hours. Decorate with mixed peel.

DELUXE CELEBRATION FRUIT CAKE

This is a rich offering full of its own importance. Small slices will suffice most hearty appetites for a sweet moment of weakness. Give in to it, go celebrate!

75 g (3 oz) currants
75 g (3 oz) raisins
75 g (3 oz) sultanas
75 g (3 oz) glacé cherries
75 g (3 oz) mixed peel
250 ml (8 fl oz) orange juice
25 g (1 oz) chopped mixed nuts
2 pieces chopped stem ginger
150 ml (¼ pt) semi-skimmed milk
55 ml (2 fl oz) vegetable oil
225 g (8 oz) whole meal self-raising flour
10 g (2 tsp) mixed spice
45 ml (3 tbsp) cognac
Apricot jam, for glazing
Glacé fruits to decorate.

Put the currants, raisins, sultanas, cherries and peel into a large bowl and blend in the orange juice. Cover with Clingfilm and leave to soak overnight. The next day, pre-heat the oven to 150C/300F/gas mark 2. Take a deep cake tin – either 20 cm (8") round or 18 cm (7") square – grease and line with greaseproof paper. Add chopped mixed nuts and ginger to the fruit mixture; stir in milk and oil; sift flour and mixed spice into it also, and finally add the cognac. Spoon mixture into the cake tin and bake in oven for about 90-100 minutes, or until cake is firm to the touch. Turn out and cool on a wire rack. Brush with sieved apricot jam and decorate with glacé fruits.

'Do it when you can
Anywhere you can
Anytime at all
Just do it!'

From 'Do it'
K. Clayton

Caribbean Chicken Kebabs

ACT SIX

BRILLIANT BARBIES

My sunshine chapter. Mastering the art of the barbecue takes patience and protective gloves! I speak from singed experience. Once a uniquely American and Australian outdoor tradition, barbecuing has become a popular element of the British summer season. Terry, my associate chef, is Australian (very!) and he has buffed-up my barbie know-how no end.

It's great to get out, cook out and eat out. Your garden is another room, treat it that way. In England, of course, we are at the mercy of the weather. Ensure back-up arrangements and keep your sense of humour close at hand. I remember, years ago, a barbecue that could have been scripted by Mel Brooks.

The day had been brilliantly sunny until the moment of cooking arrived. The heavens opened. *He*, hastily throwing a brolly at *her*, retired inside. *She* steadfastly remained at the helm of her spluttering barbie. Spurning the brolly in the true Brit tradition of 'it's just a few spots', *she* stood resolute, drenched in the force 10 Niagara and went on to persevere and create a dish now affectionately known in our circles as *Noah's Ark soaked and soiled Steak*.

She was wearing a very, very short crocheted frock at the start. *She* stood heroically against the elements but her shorty was not up to the challenge. *We* stood steadfastly indoors and watched, fascinated. The wetter and wider the crochet, the longer – and lower – it stretched until it reached past her ankles and began to assemble in soggy folds on the patio deck. The resultant 're-design' was, to say the least, revealing! Gathering the steaks together *she* turned imperiously and, with true British aplomb, fell over her new long dress and, with the steaks, burgers and all, dived headfirst into a flower bed. Rising with slow dignity and a face full of wet earth and burger bits she said, 'Anyone fancy a take-away?'

For a successful barbecue you don't necessarily need a garden. Barbie on the patio, a terrace, a roof or your balcony if you have sympathetic neighbours (if your neighbours are invitable, that solves *that* problem).

Terry prefers a built-in barbecue. Built-in barbies, blending in with your garden, are easily constructed out of rocks or brick and cement, with a concealing low wall acting as a windbreak. Metal shelves, grills and work surface are incorporated into the structure. As the seasons change, cover your shelves and grills, and your summer outdoor kitchen can become a winter repository for plants. There are numerous, environmentally friendly barbecue systems available on the market, including some inexpensive portables.

Saturday or Sunday barbecues are best. Guests can come and go (one of the practical aspects of barbies), time pressures are at a minimum. Pre-prepared marinades done the night before help. A couple of meat dishes* and one seafood should be sufficient. Accompany with jacket potatoes, pasta or deluxe, all-in salad and a pot-pourri of pickles and relishes.

***FIZZTIP:** A word about meat.
Australians would find barbecues unthinkable without beef. My Fizzical recipes tend to avoid red meat because it is high in fat and cholesterol. Your own judgement and fitness goals come into play here, but do remember there are other meats, not to mention fish, which are completely at home on the barbie grill. I hope you'll find something new and delicious in the following recipes which include poultry, pork and seafood. Don't forget the best fish for barbecuing are the oily ones (mackerel, herrings, sardines, trout or salmon).

And now, a word about your equipment. There is a vast array of barbecue gadgetry available nowadays but, again, my motto is less is more. The essentials are:

Tongs – a good long-handled pair so your nail polish doesn't melt. **Hinged long handled grill** – this double-sided little device holds the food between two layers of mesh. Vital for fish and burgers.

Long-handled fork – for turning bulky items of meat.

Basting brush – again, a long-handled one for coating food with marinades.

Aluminium foil – cooking in foil 'packets' is a splendid way of preparing small items (such as fish fillets) which could otherwise stick to, or slide through, the grill.

All other necessary cooking accoutrements ought to be available in your kitchen.

Finally, a word about marinades. It is a well-known fact that a good marinade tenderises meat and makes it even better for grilling, and a baste is essential to keep the meat moist whilst cooking. When the food, drink and ambience blend well on such an occasion, you'll know your barbecue is a success. Your guests will relax, read the papers, play games, take a nap. Sounds good to me! Go on, Tel, throw another prawn on the barbie ...z-z-z-zzz...

- BRILLIANT BARBIES -

(All recipes 6-8 servings)

CARIBBEAN CHICKEN KEBABS

Tel insists this is an authentic taste of the Caribbean. Authentic taste of Sydney is my guess. Whatever, he assures me they go down well with barbie freaks so best make sure there's plenty to go around.

60 ml (4 tbsp) freshly squeezed lime juice
Grated rind from two of the limes
30 ml (2 tbsp) dry sherry
30 ml (2 tbsp) honey
10 g (2 tsp) ground cinnamon
1.35 kg (3 lbs) boneless, skinless chicken breasts
4 mangoes, peeled and cubed
18-24 button mushrooms, washed and dried

In a large bowl, mix together the lime juice and rind, sherry, honey and cinnamon. Cut the chicken into bite-sized chunks and place in the bowl of marinade for 2-3 hours, or overnight in the fridge. Thread chicken pieces on to wooden or metal kebab skewers, alternating with the mango cubes and button mushrooms. Grind black pepper over the prepared kebabs, place on a hot barbecue grill for 8-10 minutes, turning occasionally and basting with the marinade.

MIXED GRILL KEBABS

This is one for the fellas with hearty appetites.

2 chicken breasts, cubed
Shallots, peeled but left whole
2-3 lean pork steaks, cubed
2-3 lean bacon chops, cubed
Red peppers, cut into small squares
5 ml (1 tsp) soy sauce
30 ml (2 tbsp) dry sherry

Alternating chicken, shallots, pork, pepper and bacon, thread them on to the required number of wooden or metal kebab skewers. In a small bowl, mix the soy sauce with the sherry and, as the kebabs cook on the barbecue, brush with the glaze. Turn kebabs occasionally until all meat begins to brown. Serve immediately.

KING PRAWN and GINGER KEBABS

It's hard to beat the combination of spicy fresh ginger and king prawns. Serve with Barbecue Jacket Potatoes or the Tomato and Red Onion Salad with Pistachios (see p. 174)

30 ml (2 tbsp) tomato purée
30 ml (2 tbsp) white rum
30 ml (2 tbsp) honey
15 ml (1 tbsp) soy sauce
15 g (1 tbsp) freshly grated root ginger
1 heaped tsp dried ginger
1.35 kg (3lbs) shelled king prawns
2 large Spanish onions, quartered & cut into bite-size pieces
1 pineapple, peeled, cored and cut into bite-size cubes
Ground black pepper
Chopped parsley for garnish

In a bowl, mix together the puree, rum, honey, soy sauce, fresh and dried ginger. Marinate the prawns in the mixture overnight, or for minimum 3 hours before cooking. Thread the prawns on to wooden or metal skewers, alternating with the onion pieces and pineapple cubes. Grind black pepper over the kebabs and barbecue for 8-10 minutes, brushing with the marinade and turning occasionally. Garnish with chopped parsley.

MARINATED CHICKEN LEGS

These work wonderfully with dips such as Avocado dip with Lemon and Spring Onion (see p.56).

20 chicken legs, skinned and scored
30 ml (2 tbsp) vegetable oil
30 ml (2 tbsp) soy sauce
30 ml (2 tbsp) honey
30 ml (2 tbsp) dry sherry
1 clove garlic, crushed
15 g (1 tbsp) freshly grated root ginger

Place the chicken legs in a casserole dish. Make the marinade by combining all the other ingredients and then pour over the legs. Leave, covered with Clingfilm, overnight in the fridge. Barbecue for 8-10 minutes, turning occasionally and brushing with the marinade.

INDIAN FISH KEBABS

Why not add a taste of India to your barbecue? This has a really exotic Eastern kick to it and goes very well with cool plain cooked rice with a little turmeric and fennel seeds added.

FIZZTIP: As another accompaniment, you can also cook your own poppadams (these are widely available in supermarkets and Indian food stores and are infinitely tastier than the ready-cooked ones) on the barbecue, but you have to be nimble. Simply place on the grill, slightly overlapping the edge nearest you, and, with your fingertips, turn the poppadam around and over quickly until it bubbles and browns. It should take no more than 20-30 seconds to cook one poppadam. Leave each one to sit for a few minutes to 'crisp' before eating.

10 g (4 tsp) curry powder
30 ml (2 tbsp) tomato ketchup
½ tsp ground nutmeg
275 ml (½ pt) low-fat, natural yoghurt
900g (2 lbs) firm fish fillets, such as cod or halibut, skinned and cubed
6 firm bananas, cut into 2.5 cm (1") chunks
1 pineapple, peeled and with flesh cut into 2.5 cm (1") chunks
Paprika

In a bowl, make your marinade by mixing the curry powder, ketchup, nutmeg and yoghurt. Skewer the fish cubes, alternating with banana and pineapple pieces, place the kebabs in a flat dish and the pour marinade over them. Store in the fridge under Clingfilm overnight. Barbecue for 8-10 minutes, turning and basting occasionally with the marinade. Sprinkle on a little paprika for an extra kick.

SPICY VEGGIE BURGER

Yes, there is life for a vegetarian at a barbecue. Or simply for those desiring something a little different which satisfies on a savoury level and is also very good for you.

175 g (6 oz) dark mushrooms, wiped
and finely chopped
2 carrots, chopped
1 large Spanish onion, roughly chopped
2 courgettes, chopped
50 g (1 oz) whole almonds
1 red chilli, chopped
5 g (1 tsp) curry powder
½ tsp ground ginger
2 egg whites
1 cupful of fresh bread crumbs
45 g (3 tbsp) parsley, chopped
10 ml (2 tsp) yeast extract
Salt and freshly ground pepper
Wholemeal flour

In a non-stick frying pan, dry-fry the mushrooms for about 5-6 minutes until the moisture has evaporated. Put the carrots, onion, courgettes, almonds, chilli, curry powder, ginger and egg whites into a blender or food processor. Blend until the mixture begins to bind – probably no more than 30-40 seconds. Put the mixture into a bowl and fold in the bread crumbs, parsley, yeast and seasoning. Using the whole meal flour, shape into flat burgers (the mix should make about 6-8 thick burgers). Leave in the fridge to cool for 3-4 hours. Barbecue for about 8-10 minutes, turning once.

SALMON and MIXED PEPPER KEBABS

I have always loved the marriage of fresh salmon and peppers. Why not add cherry tomatoes to these kebabs for that extra burst of colour?

4-6 salmon steaks
Groundnut oil
2-3 firm jacket potatoes, skins-on and par-boiled to soft but not fluffy
1 red pepper, seeded and cut into 2.5 cm (1") squares
1 green pepper, seeded and cut into 2.5 cm (1") squares
2 lemons, quartered

Brush a little oil on to the steaks and grill for about 3 minutes each side. Remove from grill onto a plate and allow to cool. Meanwhile, cut the potatoes into roughly 2.5 cm (1") cubes. When the steaks have cooled, cut into bite-size chunks and skewer the pieces, alternating with the potato cubes and pepper squares. Brush the kebabs with oil, place on the barbecue and cook for about 10 minutes, turning once. Serve with lemon wedges.

FIZZTIP: Be sure to skewer the salmon chunks through the sides to stop flaking.

HAWAIIAN TURKEY BREASTS with MANGO

Paired together, tender turkey breasts and mango are a taste triumph. Outdoors on a crisp, sunny day, you'll have a 'South Pacific' hit on your hands.

3 mangoes, peeled and cut into slivers
5 g(1 tsp) ground cinnamon
½ tsp ground ginger
Finely grated rind of 2 limes
45-60 ml (3-4 tbsp) lime juice
30 ml (2 tbsp) honey (or
  equivalent sweetener)
30 ml (2 tbsp) rum
6-8 turkey breast steaks

Put the mango slivers into a small mixing bowl then sprinkle on the cinnamon and ginger; mix gently with a wooden spoon. Then add the lime rind and juice, honey or sweetener and rum; mix one more time. Score the turkey breast steaks and lay them on a flat dish. Pour the mango marinade over the breasts, cover with Clingfilm and leave in the fridge for a good hour or two. When ready to barbecue, place the steaks on to the grill, brush with the marinade (which is best placed in a small saucepan on the barbecue grill to heat), turn once or twice and, just before serving, spoon the warm marinade over each breast. Serve immediately.

BARBECUED WHOLE FISH

One has to be a little careful barbecuing a whole fish. The severity of a barbecue often sears the outside too quickly and leaves the inside underdone. This is not such a problem with meat because meat can stand a longer grilling time; indeed the charring of meat enhances its flavour when barbecues are concerned. However, you can barbecue fish successfully. Cod, haddock, mullet, trout or monkfish are all favourites.

* Don't attempt to barbecue extremely large fish, or any fish thicker than a maximum of 4 cm (1½").

* Heat-up your double-sided hinged-grill over the barbecue – this will help prevent fish sticking to it. Clean the fish, brush both sides fully with a little olive oil and freshly milled black pepper. Grill over hot coals (try to avoid flames) for about 15-20 minutes – according to the size of the fish – turning occasionally.

* Alternatively, part-cook the fish wrapped in foil in a

medium oven for about 15-20 minutes prior to placing on the barbecue. This way, the fish will be juicier inside. When you place the fish on the barbecue, it will only need 8-10 minutes maximum, turning once, and the skin will brown and crisp nicely.

ORANGE BACON CHOPS

The smell of bacon wafting through the air teases the taste buds – with real oranges and redcurrant jelly, this tears up the track and leaves other bacon recipes on the starting grid.

2 large sweet oranges (reserve the skin of one for the rind)
75 ml (3 fl oz) redcurrant jelly
Freshly ground black pepper
6-8 lean bacon chops
10 g (2 tsp) orange rind, grated
15 g (1 tbsp) parsley, finely chopped

Remove the peel and pith from the oranges and carefully remove the segments (do this over a pan so you catch the orange juice). Put the segments into the pan with the redcurrant jelly and some pepper. Simmer over a medium heat until the segments are soft and the liquid reduced. Grill the bacon chops on the barbecue for about 8-10 minutes, turning once. Meanwhile, put the rind and parsley into a small bowl and mix thoroughly. Put the orange and redcurrant mixture into a small jug and pour over the chops when cooked, finishing off with a sprinkling of the rind and parsley mixture.

GINGER PORK STEAKS

I call this my Fred and Ginger recipe. It was on the menu at the studio when they made the film 'Frying Down to Rio'.

30 ml (2 tbsp) lemon juice
30 ml (2 tbsp) honey
10 ml (2 tsp) soy sauce
10 g (2 tsp) grated fresh ginger
Freshly ground black pepper
4 lean pork steaks

In a bowl, mix together the lemon juice, honey, soy sauce, ginger and black pepper. Then score each steak with a sharp knife (not too deeply). Pour over marinade and let sit for an hour or two in the fridge. When ready to cook, simply place on the barbecue and, brushing with the marinade mixture, cook for about 8-10 minutes, turning occasionally.

FRUITS-OF-THE-SEA PARCELS

A clever little Australian dish which makes a deliciously light starter or a substantial main course for anything from a barbie to a posh dinner party, outdoors or in.

900 g (2 lbs) mixed, cubed, white fish fillets
(cod, haddock or monkfish are perfect)
1 large orange (segments and rind)
2 limes (juice and rind)
15 g (1 tbsp) fresh rosemary
5 g (1 tsp) ground nutmeg
15-20 seedless sweet grapes
10-12 cherry tomatoes
Sea salt and black pepper
White wine

Grease six generous squares of foil with a little vegetable oil. Divide the fish cubes into 6 portions and lay them on each square. With a grater, remove the rind from the oranges and limes, then squeeze the juice from the limes into a small bowl. Add the rind from both fruits and mix lightly along with the rosemary and nutmeg. Dot the grapes, tomatoes and orange segments on to each fish portion. Lift the foil edges to retain the liquid and add a few drops of white wine, sprinkle with a little sea salt and pepper. Finally, fold foil over each portion – like a parcel – allowing generous space for the ingredients to 'breathe' during cooking – and seal well. Place on the grill and allow 20-25 minutes to cook. When ready, place each parcel on to a plate, open the foil and eat immediately.

SUNSHINE SARDINES with RATATOUILLE

A sunny combination bringing the Mediterranean on to your plate.

16-20 fresh sardines
30 ml (2 tbsp) olive oil
Sea salt and black pepper
60 ml (4 tbsp) low-fat natural yoghurt
Garlic clove, crushed
Juice of ½ lemon
60 g (4 tbsp) chopped, mixed fresh
herbs of your choice

Begin by cleaning the sardines under cold running water. Let them dry on a plate, then brush them with the oil. Sprinkle sea salt and freshly milled black pepper over the fish and put to one side. Next, in a small bowl mix together the remaining ingredients, cover and put into the fridge for at least an hour. Place the sardines side by side on the pre-heated (over the coals) double-sided hinged grill and barbecue for 8-10 minutes, turning once. Serve with the yoghurt mixture on the side and accompany with a bowl of ratatouille.

- SIDE ORDERS -

MIXED VEGETABLE and RICE SALAD

In the past, some of my guests have eaten a full plate of this wonderful combination salad, then a second, and never got around to the barbie! Experience has now taught me to present it as a pièce-de-résistance.

450 g (1 lb) brown long-grain rice, cooked
4 celery stalks, sliced into 5 mm (¼") pieces
4-6 spring onions, chopped
225 g (8 oz) petit pois, cooked and cooled
225 g (8 oz) corn kernels, cooked and cooled
2 red peppers, seeded and finely chopped
50 g (2 oz) flaked almonds
100 g (4 oz) stoned dates, chopped
45 ml (3 tbsp) vegetable oil
45 ml (3 tbsp) apple juice
30 ml (2 tbsp) wine vinegar
10 g (2 tsp) curry powder
2 garlic cloves, crushed

Mix together the rice, celery, onions, petit pois, corn, peppers, almonds and dates. In a jar, shake together the oil, apple juice, vinegar, curry powder and garlic. Before serving, pour dressing over salad and toss thoroughly.

SPRING GREEN PASTA SALAD

Presentation is all important – especially in the garden. When your guests feast their eyes on this easy-to-prepare but elaborate spring green salad, with the addition of spinach pasta, they'll know they're in good company – yours.

700 g (1½ lbs) tagliatelle verdi (green) pasta, cooked and drained in cold water
1 Cos lettuce, torn into small pieces
225 g (8 oz) spinach leaves
1 cucumber, thinly sliced
2-3 celery sticks, sliced lengthways into thin 5 cm (2") sticks
2 leeks, washed, sliced lengthways into 5 cm (2") strips (with layers separated)
30 ml (2 tbsp) olive oil
10 ml (2 tsp) balsamic vinegar
15-20 ml (2 tbsp) honey (or equivalent sweetener)
Basil leaves to garnish

Toss all ingredients – except oil, vinegar and honey – in a large salad bowl. In a jar, shake the oil, vinegar and honey or sweetener and just before serving, pour on to the salad. Scatter basil leaves on top.

NOSH-TRALIAN ALL-IN SALAD

Basically, this is a salad combining greens, vegetables, fruits, nuts, (and optional bolts from Sydney Harbour Bridge) but with an emphasis on firm ingredients. This is Tel's favourite. The combination is terrific whichever way you choose to chop your chunks.

Celery chunks
Cherry tomatoes
Cucumber chunks
Fennel root slices
Red onion rings
Carrot slices, thin
Green grapes, seedless and whole
Black olives, stoned
Whole toasted almond slivers
Walnut pieces
Sultanas
Sweet corn kernels
15 g (1 tbsp) fresh ginger, grated

Place all the ingredients into a salad bowl. Because this all-in salad boasts a vast range and cross-section of tastes, add the simplest possible salad dressing or just some olive oil and a little white wine vinegar, with sea salt and pepper to taste.

BARBECUE JACKET POTATOES

King Edward, Maris Piper and Desiree are all perfect for jacket potatoes. Allow one good-size potato per person. Wrap in foil, par-bake in the oven for about 30 minutes at 200C/400F/gas mark 6. Transfer to the barbecue coals and leave to cook for another 15-20 minutes. To serve, leave the foil intact, cut a deep cross through each potato, fold back the foil, fluff up the centre with a fork, insert generous portion of low-fat spread and season to taste. Alternatively, use yoghurt with chopped chives and spring onions – delicious!

OILED CORN-ON-THE-COB with TURMERIC

Allow one fresh corn-on-the-cob per person; remove the outer leaves and string, slice off both ends, brush with corn oil and sprinkle all over with turmeric. Grill on the barbecue for 10-12 minutes, turning frequently. Lavish with freshly ground black pepper.

TOMATO and RED ONION SALAD with PISTACHIO NUTS

A popular favourite and perfect for a summer's day. Simply slice beef tomatoes, place a layer in a flat serving dish, then put a layer of finely sliced red onion rings on top, followed by a handful of shelled pistachio nuts. Repeat the process until you have the required amount for your guests, then sprinkle olive oil liberally on top, along with sea salt, and finish off with some finely chopped basil leaves.

NEW POTATO SALAD BOWL with FROMAGE FRAIS DRESSING

New potatoes, especially when in season, make the most delightful salad. The blending of tastes and textures in this salad will always satisfy.

900 g (2 lbs) new potatoes
15 ml (1 tbsp) honey (or equivalent sweetener)
Small tub of fromage frais
15 ml (1 tbsp) white wine vinegar
Paprika
Salt and pepper to taste
2 medium carrots, finely grated
3-4 spring onions, finely chopped
1 bunch watercress
3-4 Iceberg lettuce leaves
Chopped chives

Wash then boil the new potatoes until soft but leave the skins intact (depending on size of the potatoes, this should take about 8-10 minutes). When cooked, plunge the potatoes into a bowl of cold water immediately to stop them cooking further. Put aside. In a jar, shake together the honey or sweetener, fromage frais, vinegar, a little paprika, salt and pepper until thoroughly mixed. When the potatoes have cooled, strain and put them into a mixing bowl. With a wooden spoon, carefully add the grated carrot, chopped spring onions and watercress. Now transfer the whole mixture into a serving bowl lined with the lettuce leaves. Finally, trickle dressing over salad and garnish with chives.

GREEN LENTIL, PEANUT and CABBAGE SALAD

A warm crunchy salad that complements any barbecued meat dish. Best served freshly made with a just a few minutes to cool before serving.

275 g (10 oz) green lentils
1 large onion (studded with 6 cloves)
2 bay leaves
Salt and pepper
2-3 tbsp olive oil
1 large red onion, peeled and finely sliced
275 g (10 oz) firm cabbage, finely grated
115 g (4 oz) unsalted fresh peanuts
15 ml (1 tbsp) fennel seeds
Red wine vinegar
Juice of 1 large orange

Rinse the lentils in cold water, then transfer to a large pan with enough water to cover them. Add the onion with cloves and bay leaves. Season to taste with salt and pepper. Bring to boil and cook for about 10 minutes. Lower the heat, put the lid on the pan and simmer gently for a further 20 minutes. When cooked, drain and remove the onion and bay leaves. In a large frying pan, heat the olive oil and add the red onion. Cook for about 5 minutes until soft. Add the cabbage, peanuts and fennel seeds. Cook for a further 5-7 minutes until the cabbage is tender but still crunchy. Finally, stir in the cooked lentils, place in a serving bowl and finish off with a few drops of vinegar and the orange juice.

- PS: MARINADES -

Here are three of my favourite barbecue marinades, which all work equally well with fish or meat dishes. They can be prepared well in advance. In each case, pour over the meat or fish you intend to marinade and keep in the fridge overnight under Clingfilm.

GINGER and SOY

30 ml (2 tbsp) olive oil
60 ml (4 tbsp) light or dark soy sauce
15 ml (1 tbsp) red wine vinegar
5 g (1 tsp) freshly ground ginger
1 crushed garlic clove
30 ml (2 tbsp) honey (or equivalent sweetener)

Mix all ingredients together in a bowl.

ORANGE JUICE and PARSLEY

125 ml (4 fl oz) freshly squeezed orange juice
60 ml (2 tbsp) tomato ketchup (or 1 tbsp tomato purée)

- 2-3 heaped tablespoons of freshly chopped parsley
- 30 ml (2 tbsp) lemon juice
- 15 ml (1 tbsp) Worcestershire sauce

Mix all ingredients together in a bowl.

LEMON and ONION

- Juice of 3-4 lemons
- 45 ml (3 tbsp) olive oil
- 30-45 ml (2-3 tbsp) chopped spring onion
- 15 ml (1 tbsp) honey (or equivalent sweetener)
- Sea salt and black pepper to taste

Mix all ingredients together in a bowl.

'It's time to think about thinking
What you think, how you think,
how you live
Set your mind, you will find
you can change it
There's so much to receive
and to give'

From 'The Fizz'
Margolis/Clayton

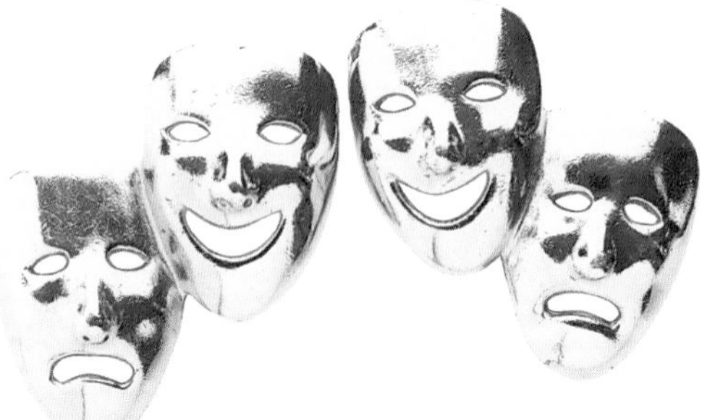

INTERVAL

FIZZICAL SLIMMING YOUR 7 DAY FATBURNER

Let yourself go? Feeling low? Lost incentive? Missing out on that 10-20 minute workout each morning? No swim? No gym? No slim? No win!

Okay. Strip off! Bikini on! Mirror test.

Look at yourself. What do you see? This is it!

We have a song lyric for this moment;

> 'This is it right now, there's no way out
> This is it right now, you'd better look out
> Where you are where you're at, there's
> no doubt about that
> Do you wanna know when, do you
> wanna know how?'

From 'This is it Right Now!'
Margolis/Clayton

It's right NOW! Go to the fridge and store cupboard. Give away all forbidden things. Cream, butter, full-fat milks, biscuits, bread, carbonated drinks, alcohol (well, put it in the cupboard under the stairs and give someone else the key).

This INTERVAL section is about turning your home into a health farm for just seven days.

It's about DISCIPLINE. Declining dinner or luncheon party invitations. Changing your entire eating policy for just one week. It's a little discipline for a lot of result. And, with stick-to-it-ness you will find the results of this chapter truly amazing and joyously rewarding. If you have any ailments or illnesses, show this chapter to your doctor before you launch into this seven day eating programme.

THE FIZZICAL 7 DAY FATBURNER

How to lose 10-15 lbs safely in a week

When you embark on this eating programme. Keep this book in your kitchen and refer to this section every day. Before you start – read this entire section.

There are many international variations on this fast track eating programme which literally 'burns away' the fat. This one is medically approved, completely safe and similar diets are used in heart hospitals from Luton to Los Angeles. Its method is to burn more calories than you take in. It flushes impurities from your system, clamps down on cholesterol and will zap you with improved energy levels and a feel-good factor you can actually feel. I'm afraid alcohol is out until 24 hours after you have completed the programme (this is because of the fat-removal 'build down' which will be happening in your system). This is the eating programme that reduced my husband to cheers! In 7 days, Mike lost 14lbs. to the ounce. But he stuck to the system and so can you.

Okay, here we go. We begin with the soup.

Fatburner Soup

6 large spring onions
2 green peppers
1 bunch of celery
1 head of cabbage
1 large pack of spinach
1 head of broccoli
1 pack of purple sprouting
(whenever you can get it in season)
2 carrots
3 leeks
6 small mushrooms
1 or 2 400 g (14 oz) tins of plum tomatoes
1 large onion

Season, if desired, with sea salt, freshly ground black pepper, curry powder or paste, parsley, Tabasco, Soy or other hot sauce, to taste. Garlic is optional, as is artificial sweetener.

Preparation

Use your biggest saucepan to make enough soup. Which can be kept in the fridge, for several days. Cut vegetables into small pieces and cover with water. Bring to a rapid boil, cook for 10 minutes then reduce to simmer. Continue until all vegetables are tender. (30-40 minutes).

Whenever you are hungry you can eat this soup. Eat as much as you like, whenever you like and need to. This soup will not add calories and, though it sounds crazy, the more you eat, the more weight you will lose. Follow the diet plan instructions because if you just eat the soup on its own, your intake will be short on essential nutrients. The object of this is to become healthy, not break any records.

If you work takes you away for long periods of the day, make a flask of the soup and take it with you.

Weigh yourself once before you start the diet and then again on the morning of day 4, before continuing with the Day 4 diet and after going to the loo. Thus you will, on that morning, gauge your weight loss accurately.

Day One

All fruit except Bananas. (Watermelons and Cantaloupes are lower in calories than most other fruits). Only eat the soup and fruits. Drink: Unsweetened Tea, Cranberry Juice, Water.

Day Two

Vegetable only day. Literally stuff yourself with as much as you can reasonably pack away of fresh, raw or tinned vegetables. Eat green leaf vegetables. Do not eat dry beans, peas or corn. Eat your vegetables together with the soup. At supper time today, have one large baked potato with butter substitute. Do not eat any fruits this day.

Day Three

Eat as much soup, fruits and vegetables as you can. Sorry no baked potato today. If you have stick exactly to the diet these three days and have not deviated at all, when you weigh yourself tomorrow morning you will find that you will have lost between 5-7lbs! (After today, weigh yourself every morning.

Day Four

Banana and skimmed milk day! Eat three bananas in or with the skimmed milk and drink as many glasses of water as you can today. Yes, Bananas are high in calories and high in carbohydrates, likewise milk but today your body needs the potassium and carbohydrates, the proteins and calcium. These will also lessen any cravings for sweets. Eat the soup at least once but no veggies or salad this day.

Day Five

Beef (Yes, beef!) or chicken, or fish and tomatoes. You are allowed 10-20 oz. (275-700 g) of lean beef (or chicken or fish) and a a tin of (or 6 fresh) tomatoes today. If you can also manage 6-8 glasses of water today, it will cleanse the uric acid out of your body. Eat the soup at least once today.

Day Six

This is beef or chicken, or fish and vegetable day. Eat as much lean beef or chicken or fish and vegetables as you like today. You can even have two or three lean steaks accompanied by green leafy veggies. No baked potato. Eat the soup at least once today.

Day Seven

(Almost done!) Many say this is the hardest day but take heart – you're in sight of your final goal. Stuff yourself with cooked brown rice, unsweetened fruit juice and vegetables. Pack in as much as you can without being silly. Have the soup at least once today. And that's the seven day system done and dusted. Well done you!

Now read this – it is important to understand the following when you weigh yourself on the morning of the eighth day, providing you have disciplined yourself as per the diet instructions. You should find you have lost 10-17 lbs. (If you have shed more than 15 lbs, take a rest from this programme for two weeks before re-starting with day one).

Other than that, you can use this system as much as you like. (After the first week if you return to the diet, you can keep yourself in check by just doing he first three days). Following this diet will help rid your body of impurities and make you feel fitter and better about yourself than you have felt since your weight became a concern to you.

After the first seven days you will be and feel 10-17 lbs. lighter. Your energy levels will have increased dramatically. Continue as long as you like and want to maintain that fit feeling and look.

Don't even think about it!

No bread. No alcohol. No carbonated drinks including diet drinks. Stick it out with water, unsweetened tea, black coffee (if you must), unsweetened fruit juices, cranberry juice (excellent) and skimmed milk (you'll get used to it). Hopefully, your experience with this diet will affect your eating habits from now on. Enjoy your food. But you owe it to yourself and your loved ones to be fit and well. So think about what you eat!

Last Word

Everyone has a different digestive system, so this diet will affect everyone in an individual way. After day three, if you don't cheat, you will already have more energy than when you began. If, after several days on the diet, you find that your bowel movements have changed, eat a cup of bran or fibre with fat-free milk. You may have black coffee with this diet but after day three you no longer need that caffeine. This diet is safe for heart patients and approved for rapid wight loss without side effects. If in doubt, check it out with your doctor.

After day seven, mirror-test yourself and say:

'Hi, slim!'

'This time. The word "No" is
not an option
This time. It will be right on the night
All right!'

From 'This Time'
Margolis/Clayton

Plain and Simple Linguine with
Chopped Tomatoes

ACT SEVEN

SIMPLY SUPPERS

This is about eating late! After a performance I love to come back to a glass of wine and a stir-fry, in that order. The marvellous thing about wok cooking is that preparation can be minimal. If you've followed this book carefully, you now have a kitchen stocked with your basics. One wok and a combination of imagination, daring and speed can produce gourmet results in 10 minutes.

Supper (as distinct from dinner) should be a light evening meal taken late – perhaps with friends after the theatre, cinema, concert or a cocktail party. Many people like to eat late but it must be emphasised that the late evening meal is the one you take to bed with you and sleep with, all night. So it's best to keep it light. You won't find any recipes in this act for chicken korma, doner kebab or hamburger and chips.

Stir-fried food has a great deal going for it when it comes to suppers. It's quick, healthy, the smells instantly tickle the taste buds and it's on the plate before you can say F-F-F-Fizzical! There's a minimal amount of washing up and it doesn't lie heavily on the stomach. So, as Confucius say:

'If Sage live in cloister, the wok is his oyster.
To quickly stir-fry, make sure heat is high.
Hot wok retain goodness without any doubt
and if Sage cannot cook, Sage should eat out.'

Anyway, this act has other suggestions for suppers, all with an emphasis on delicacy and late-night nourishment. This is a lovely way to spend an evening...

- SIMPLY SUPPERS -

(All recipes 3-4 servings)

RED WINE and ORANGE CONSOMMÉ

Serve this soup garnished with fresh vegetables such as leek, spring onion or carrot cut finely into 'threads'.

Segments of 2 large oranges
(and the rind of one orange)
1 large onion, chopped
2 medium carrots, chopped
1 medium celery stick, chopped
1 bouquet garni
2 cloves
Cayenne pepper to taste
1 400 g (14 oz) tin of beef consommé
250 ml (8 fl oz) red wine

Put the orange segments, onion, carrots, celery, bouquet garni, cloves and pepper into a large saucepan; add the consommé, bring to the boil, lower the heat and very gently simmer for 20-25 minutes. Remove from the heat, cool for about 10 minutes, strain through a sieve – be sure to press the orange segments to extract any remaining juice – and return to the saucepan. Add the wine, bring to the boil again then allow to simmer uncovered for about 4-5 minutes. Garnish with the orange rind and the vegetable threads.

TOMATO, TARRAGON and RICE SOUP

10 ml (2 tsp) olive oil
1 medium onion (chopped)
1 medium potato (chopped)
700 g (1½ lbs) ripe tomatoes (skins on and quartered)
275 ml (10 fl oz) chicken stock (see p. 23)
10 ml (2 tsp) tomato purée
1 garlic clove (crushed)
5 ml (1 tsp) dried tarragon
60 ml (4 tbsp) cooked rice
Fresh tarragon for garnish
Salt and pepper to taste

Heat the oil in a heavy saucepan and sauté the onion and potato for 3-4 minutes until onions become opaque. Add tomatoes, stock, purée, garlic and dried tarragon. Bring to the boil, reduce and simmer for about 20-25 minutes. When cooked, allow to cool for 10-15 minutes, then purée in a blender or food processor. Pass through a sieve to remove pulp and tomato skins. Return to the pan, add the cooked rice and heat – but do not boil – before serving.

MONKFISH STIR-FRY

Monkfish are so called because they have some very odd habits...Monks ...! ... odd habits! ... Oh well, be that as it may, its lovely texture makes monkfish perfect for stir-frying. Superb with rice noodles.

450 g (1 lb) monkfish
15 g (1 tbsp) chopped parsley
Juice of 1 lemon
1 400 g (14 oz) tin of chopped tomatoes
30 ml (2 tbsp) groundnut oil
1 medium onion, chopped
2 celery sticks, sliced thinly
4-6 baby corn, cut lengthways
Worcestershire sauce

Remove the skin and bone from the monkfish (your fishmonger may do this for you) and cut the flesh into strips or thin chunks; marinate the fish in the parsley and lemon juice for about an hour. Drain the juice from the tinned tomatoes but keep it. Heat the oil in the wok and stir-fry the onion for 2-3 minutes. Add the fish and continue stir-frying for a further 2-3 minutes; add the tomatoes, celery, corn, and Worcestershire sauce to taste. At this point, depending on how much liquid you like in your stir-fry, pour in the tomato juice from the can and turn up the heat for a further 2-3 minutes. Serve on warmed plates immediately.

STIR-FRY HONEYED PEAS and ASPARAGUS

This is a surprisingly light dish yet full-bodied and very tasty.

15 ml (1 tbsp) walnut oil
110 g (4 oz) baby asparagus
110 g (4 oz) mange tout
Medium red onion, cut into rings
6-8 thin slices of root ginger
75 g (3 oz) canned bamboo shoots,
drained and slivered
15 ml (1 tbsp) light soy sauce
30 ml (2 tbsp) honey

Heat walnut oil in a wok. Stir-fry asparagus, mange tout, red onion and ginger on a high heat for about 2-3 minutes. Add the bamboo shoots and soy sauce and, 2-3 minutes later, the honey. Serve on a bed of plain boiled rice.

HERRINGS with BEETROOT SALAD

Looking at this recipe, you can see what's happened here. Four herrings have been at the white wine and that's why they're canned. And I also notice that the water chestnuts are sliced. I apologise on behalf of ingredients everywhere.

4 tins of herring fillets
30 ml (2 tbsp) white wine
15 ml (1 tbsp) soy sauce
2-3 cooked beetroot
150 ml (5 oz) Greek yoghurt
Chopped chives
5 ml (1 tsp) honey (or equivalent sweetener)
10 ml (2 tbsp) olive oil
1 red pepper, seeded and chopped
3-4 spring onions, sliced
60 g (2 oz) bean sprouts
A few sliced water chestnuts

Firstly, slice the herrings into 2.5 cm (1") lengths and marinate them in the wine and soy sauce for about an hour. Then prepare the salad by cutting the beetroot into thin strips. Place in a bowl to chill. For the dressing, combine the yoghurt, chives and honey or sweetener – keeping some chives back for garnish. Next, heat the oil in a wok and stir–fry the pepper for 1-2 minutes. Add the spring onions, bean sprouts, water chestnuts and herrings with the marinade and cook for a further 2-3 minutes over a high heat. Serve with the beetroot salad and a dollop of the yoghurt dressing on the side of each plate.

CHINESE GINGER PORK with SHERRY

A novel way to eat this dish is wrapped with rice in lettuce leaves (the ginger pork, that is – not you).

450 g (1 lb) fillet of pork, cut into strips
15 g (1 tbsp) corn flour
½ tsp ginger powder
6-8 thin strips root ginger
2 cloves garlic, crushed
30 ml (2 tbsp) walnut oil
1 large Spanish onion, finely chopped
2 medium carrots, peeled and cut into
   2.5 cm (1") by 5 mm (1/4") strips
15 ml (1 tbsp) light soy sauce
5 ml (1 tsp) honey (or equivalent sweetener)
30-45 ml (2-3 tbsp) medium dry sherry

Place the pork in a small bowl, add the corn flour, ginger powder, root ginger and garlic and gently mix together; leave for at least 30 minutes. Heat the oil and stir-fry half of the pork mixture (don't put it all in together as it might stick), separating the pork pieces as you go, for about 3 minutes. Drain and put aside, then stir-fry the rest of the pork mixture for the same time. Drain, and put aside. Add the onion, carrots, soy sauce and honey or sweetener to the wok and cook on a high heat for 2-3 minutes. Return the pork to the wok, add the sherry, and cook all on a medium heat for another 2-3 minutes. Serve immediately.

STIR-FRY NOODLES with VEGETABLES

Here's your starter for ten. What is the Chinese for stir-fry noodles? Answer: chow mein. Not many people know that, aside of course from eight billion Chinese. 'Chow' means stir-fry and 'mein' means noodles. Here is a basic recipe with some exotic vegetables – including Thai pak-choi cabbage which is truly delicious and is increasingly becoming available in larger supermarkets, as well as Far Eastern specialist stores.

350 g (12 oz) basic Chinese noodles or rice noodles
30 ml (2 tbsp) walnut oil
1 Thai pak-choi cabbage, chopped into small pieces (if hard to come by, use English green cabbage)
225 g (8 oz) fresh bean sprouts
45-60 g (3-4 tbsp) canned lychees (keep syrup)

30-45 g (2-3 tbsp) slivered bamboo shoots
1 red pepper, seeded and cut into
  2.5 cm (1") strips
15 ml (1 tbsp) light soy sauce

Parboil the basic noodles in a saucepan of boiling water for 5 minutes (for rice noodles, 3 minutes); drain and put to one side. In a wok, heat the oil and add the pak-choy cabbage, bean sprouts, lychees, bamboo shoots and pepper. Stir-fry for 2-3 minutes on high, turn down the heat and add the noodles, soy sauce and a little of the lychee syrup. A further 2-3 minutes on high should be sufficient. Serve immediately.

STIR-FRY CHILLI KING PRAWNS

2 small dried red chillies
1 fresh green chilli
450 g (1 lb) king prawns, shelled, washed and drained
1 egg white
15 ml (1 tbsp) dry sherry
15 g (1 tbsp) corn flour
150 ml (5 oz) sunflower oil
2-3 slices fresh root ginger, finely chopped
1 medium onion, finely chopped
15 ml (1 tbsp) red wine vinegar
15 ml (1 tbsp) tomato purée
30 g (2 tbsp) finely chopped mixed nuts

First, chop the chillies, discarding seeds. Place the prawns in a bowl, add egg white, sherry and corn flour and mix well. Heat half the oil in a wok, add the prawns and stir-fry on a medium heat for about 2 minutes. Remove and drain. Add the rest of the oil to the wok and turn up the heat. Add the ginger and onion, cook for 2 minutes then add the vinegar and purée. Return prawns to the wok and cook all ingredients for another 2-3 minutes maximum. Sprinkle chopped nuts on top and serve immediately. Delicious served on a bed of shredded Cos lettuce and finely sliced celery, or with rice.

STIR-FRY MUSHROOMS, CABBAGE and BEAN SPROUTS

Another light evening supper dish, the crunch of the cabbage and bean sprouts blending perfectly with the dark mushrooms. This goes well with a simple grilled chicken breast.

450 g (1 lb) Chinese white cabbage
4-6 large open-cap mushrooms, dark-brown variety
Sunflower oil
225 g (8 oz) fresh bean sprouts
60 ml (4 tbsp) vegetable consommé
10 ml (2 tsp) light soy sauce
5 ml (1 tsp) sesame oil

Cut cabbage into 5 x 6 cm (2" x 2½") slices. Roughly chop the mushrooms into bite-size chunks. Heat the sunflower oil in the wok, put in cabbage and mushrooms and stir-fry for 1-2 minutes. Add the bean sprouts, consommé and soy sauce, cook on high for a further 1-2 minutes. Serve on warmed plates, sprinkling on the sesame oil as you go.

MARINATED CHICKEN BREASTS with SHALLOTS and CORIANDER

This dish is a treat served on a bed of washed and finely shredded fresh spinach mingled with fresh bean sprouts. This is where pre-prep comes into its own. It's vital to marinate this one for at least 10 hours.

4 small skinned chicken breasts
60 ml (4 tbsp) olive oil
Juice of two lemons
275 ml (10 fl oz) dry sherry or white wine
6-8 shallots, skinned and finely sliced
15 g (1 tbsp) coriander seeds, crushed
  in a pestle and mortar
15 ml (1 tbsp) vegetable oil
Fresh coriander for garnish

Generously score the chicken breasts, allowing the marinade to penetrate, and place them side by side in a casserole dish. In a jug, mix together the olive oil, lemon juice, sherry or wine, shallots and crushed coriander. Pour over the chicken, cover with Clingfilm and marinate in the fridge for a good 10-12 hours. When ready to cook, heat the oil in a frying pan or wok, extract the chicken from the marinade and cook for about 5 minutes on each side until they begin to brown. Slowly add the marinade and continue cooking on high until reduced – about another 5 minutes. Garnish with chopped fresh coriander.

MUSSELS and HALIBUT PILAF

Pilaf, or pilau, originated in Turkey and means a dish consisting of rice, flavoured with spices and cooked in stock to which meat, poultry or seafood may be added. This one is terribly easy and wonderfully tasty.

10 ml (2 tsp) olive oil
275 g (10 oz) basmati rice
5 g (1 tsp) turmeric
1 red pepper, seeded and diced
1 large onion, chopped
2 sticks celery, sliced into 2 cm/¾" pieces
150 ml (¼ pt) dry white wine
425 ml (½ pt) fish stock (see p.24)
150 g (5 oz) small button mushrooms, halved
450 g (I lb) fresh halibut, cubed
16 fresh mussels, in their shells
Salt and pepper to taste

In a large frying pan (preferably non-stick) heat the oil and fry the uncooked rice and turmeric for about 5 minutes, until the rice is opaque and the turmeric is evenly absorbed and the rice is coloured a rich golden brown. Add the pepper, onion and celery, stir in the wine and stock and bring to the boil. Reduce the heat and add the mushrooms and halibut. Cover and simmer for about 20 minutes until the rice is tender and all the liquid is absorbed (you may need a little more

water if the rice is still crunchy). Finally, stir in the mussels, salt and pepper to taste and transfer to a warmed serving dish. Serve immediately, ideally with a simple green salad. Remember, if the mussels haven't opened naturally, don't eat them.

SPECIAL BASMATI FRIED RICE

Basmati is often referred to as 'the prince of rice' (or, as we in showbiz call him, Tim) and is used almost exclusively in Indian cuisine. It is easy to cook, light, fluffy and perfect as a basis for any number of meat or vegetarian dishes.

350 g (12 oz) basmati rice
45 ml (3 tbsp) olive oil
2-3 cinnamon sticks
4-6 cardamom pods
3 medium onions, finely chopped
2 green chillies, seeds removed,
 and finely chopped
½ tsp turmeric
30 g (2 tbsp) sultanas or raisins

Start by cooking the basmati rice. There are many ways of doing this, but the quickest and simplest for this recipe is to merely sprinkle the rice into a large saucepan of boiling water, lower the heat to simmering, give it a stir and cover. Gently simmer for about 8-10 minutes. Test by eating a few grains from a fork - it should be soft on the outside but maintain a very slight crunch. Don't overcook – remember, it still has to be fried. Drain the rice thoroughly through a sieve, washing immediately under cold water to remove any starch. Put to one side. In a large pan or wok, heat the oil, add the cinnamon and cardamom, let them sizzle for 30 seconds then add onions, chillies and turmeric. Cook for about 3-4 minutes, until onions begin to brown. Add the rice and sultanas or raisins and continue stir-frying until the rice is heated through.

WARM HALIBUT SALAD with CORIANDER and SESAME DRESSING

Cod, monkfish or turbot are equally effective for this dish – all are good and fleshy, and high in oil content.

700 g (1½ lbs) halibut, skinned and cubed
225 g (8 oz) mange tout
2 heads of Lollo Rosso lettuce
3 medium carrots, cut into juliennes
175 g (6 oz) button mushrooms, sliced thinly
6-8 black olives, sliced

For the dressing:

Juice of two lemons
10 g (2 tsp) grain mustard
15 ml (1 tbsp) olive oil
90 ml (3 tbsp) sesame oil
5 g (1 tsp) coriander seeds, crushed in a pestle & mortar
15 g (1 tbsp) fresh chopped coriander

Mix all the dressing ingredients – except one tablespoon of the sesame oil – together in bowl, place halibut cubes into a shallow dish and pour on half the dressing. Marinate for at least 1 hour. Cook the mange tout in boiling water for 2-3 minutes, rinse under cold running water to prevent further cooking and place in a salad bowl along with torn lettuce, carrots, mushrooms and olives; toss thoroughly with the other half of the dressing and arrange on 3-4 individual plates. Next, drain the fish cubes and stir-fry them in the remaining sesame oil in a frying pan or wok for 6-8 minutes, stirring gently. When golden, remove the fish from the pan immediately and, with metal tongs, place equally on the individual salad portions. Garnish with chopped coriander.

PLAIN & SIMPLE LINGUINE with CHOPPED TOMATOES

Red tomatoes make a colourful palette with linguine (a sort of Hurdy-Gurdy liguine verdi) for this appetising dish. A starrier aria. You can buy fresh linguine anywhere, which cooks in a few minutes, but dried is also fine although cooking time is a little longer.

30 ml (2 tbsp) olive oil
15 ml (1 tbsp) tomato purée
2-3 spring onions, finely chopped
30 ml (2 tbsp) fresh basil, chopped
450 g (16 oz) linguine verdi, cooked and drained
450 g (16 oz) tin of chopped tomatoes, drained

Pour the oil into a large non-stick pan or wok, heat, add the purée, onions and basil. Sizzle for about 30 seconds, then add the pasta. Stir thoroughly with a wooden spoon to make sure pasta is well covered with the oil mixture. Add the chopped tomatoes and continue stirring until the sauce begins to bubble. Serve immediately.

SMOKED TROUT with MINTED PINK GRAPEFRUIT

A cool blend of savoury fish and tangy fruit, ideal for spring or summer suppers. Sensational if accompanied by boiled new potatoes.

½ a Cos lettuce
½ half a Lollo Rosso lettuce
15 ml (1 tbsp) fresh lime juice
30 g (2 tbsp) chopped fresh mint
450 g (1 lb) smoked trout, skinned, boned and sliced
2 pink grapefruit, peeled, pith removed and in segments
15 g (1 tbsp) toasted flaked almonds
Mayo frais (see p. 58)

In a salad bowl, toss together both the Cos and Lollo Rosso lettuce, lime juice and 1 tablespoon of chopped mint. Arrange on plates and place smoked trout and grapefruit among the leaves; sprinkle with almonds. In a separate small bowl, mix the mayo frais with the remaining tablespoon of mint and dollop a spoonful on the side of each plate for dipping.

'Take a step to the side
Leave ut all behind for a
moment in time
Take a step to the side!'

From 'Take a Step to the Side'
Margolis/Clayton

Valentine Red Salad

ACT EIGHT

DINNER À DEUX

A romantic candlelit dinner for two. A soirée for spooners and swooners. I love it. My introduction to the fitness video makes the following point: 'The fact that you're out there watching me means (1) you care about exercise and (2) you have put a little time aside to care for yourself'. Dinner à Deux is about putting time aside. Time for each other. Très important.

The goal is romance so plan your meal and atmosphere with attention to detail. First, turn off the television – better yet, remove the fuse! Disconnect the telephone. Start off with any of the champagne blends from Act One.

Music? Subtle. A little pianistic Cole Porter rarely fails. A menu that's light in texture and h-e-a-v-y in inference is what you're after (there are 16 sexy suggestions in this Act). You will see I avoid power spices and strong flavours for your night alone-together. Someone once said, or if they didn't they should have:

'when breaths are destined to co-mingle, two should consume the same food or stay single.'

Garlic's fine, but definitely not for one out of two.

FIZZTALE: When my man and I were first courting we both had heavy early morning schedules and used to eat out a great deal. He would bring me home to my door, bid a romantic goodnight and leave. Five minutes later, on the button, the doorbell would ring. I would open up and there was Mike, de-romanced and suffused with the appearance of unwell: 'Could I use your bathroom?' He would then lock himself away for twenty minutes, emerging pale and wan. I told my best friend about this regular tactic. 'Aah,' she said sagely, 'Lovesick! he's potty about you. I'll bet that's it. Listen at the door.' With trepidation, I did and sure enough, the flattering sound of lurgy was unmistakable. I had myself a love sick suitor! Well, tickle my soufflés with a celery stick, missus! The phone rang, It was my friend. 'Well, what did you hear?' she asked eagerly. 'Sounded like moussaka to me,' I replied. It was about a year later than Mike was diagnosed as being allergic to garlic!! He assured me, however, that his love was still strong and if it would reassure me, he would maintain the occasional burp. I said there were better ways. He agreed. So, despite the Dracula protection element in many of these recipes, our home is a garlic-free zone.

FIZZTIP: Never be shy about telling your host or hostess well in advance if allergies or dislikes need to be considered. Avoid that moment of disappointment for your hosts who have been preparing all day for you, only to find you cannot eat their efforts. It's a kind idea when you are entertaining to have a 'spare' up your sleeve. In any event, always ask if allergies are a problem.

Red is my colour of romance. Red roses will be on my table, and with fingernails sparkling red from a Supernail of LA treatment, I will ease, very... very...slowly, a fresh, heart-shaped strawberry into champagne bubbling in a flute glass. I will accompany this movement with a throaty rendition of, 'I could spend my life just loving you!', and expect results! He will say something like, 'Cor!' and we're up, up and away into a delicious ripe-red tomato salad with fresh basil and a simple dressing. You can also try the thinnest pasta gently simmered and served with just enough red pesto sauce to inflame the desire for...more! Also perfect, and as light as a baby's conscience, is a salad of Radiccio and Lollo Rosso lettuce, served as a base for freshly grilled scampi or prawns.

A word about touching. Spike Milligan once said to me, 'You're a toucher. That's important. Never be afraid to touch,' then he sent me a note which I have always treasured – 'Love, light, peace. Spike'. Those three words are a good theme for Dinner à Deux, and for life.

Conversation is as important as the menu. Communication, vibes, same-wavelengths, all happen with words. Use them well. Talk about your future, plan your holidays, dream a little. Finale with the yoghurt and passion fruit! Bon soir!

- DINNER À DEUX -

(All recipes 2 servings)

CARROT and APPLE SOUP

On a cold evening when you're in front of the fire, this wholesome soup – served with chunks of warmed wholemeal or oatmeal bread – is a satisfying meal in itself. Dollop a little yoghurt into the soup just before serving.

25 g (1 oz) low-fat spread
350 g (12 oz) carrots, peeled and roughly chopped
1 small cooking apple, cored, peeled and roughly chopped
570 ml (1 pt) chicken or vegetable stock (see p.23 and 25)
2 cloves
1 bouquet garni
75 g (3 oz) Greek yoghurt or fromage frais
Chopped parsley
Freshly ground black pepper

In a saucepan, melt the low-fat spread and cook the carrots and apple for about 8-10 minutes, stirring occasionally. Pour in the stock and add the cloves and bouquet garni, bring to the boil and simmer for 30 minutes. Remove the cloves and bouquet garni. Purée the soup in a blender, return to the saucepan and add the yoghurt or fromage frais. Bring almost back to the boil and serve, sprinkling parsley on top.

TOMATO SALAD with SATSUMA DRESSING and FRESH BASIL

Extract the juice from satsumas with an old-fashioned glass hand-press juice extractor or, even better, an electric juicer. You'll need 3-4 satsumas to make the juice equivalent of one large orange. It's worth fiddling around, the taste difference is delish!

2 medium ripe tomatoes, sliced
Segments of 2 satsumas, peeled and pithed
Juice of 3-4 satsumas
Olive oil
Fresh basil, chopped
Freshly ground black pepper

Divide the tomato slices between two medium-sized dinner plates, arrange the satsuma segments on top, then drizzle satsuma juice over them followed, in the same manner, by the olive oil. Sprinkle chopped basil over the two plates and finally add the ground black pepper.

PASTA with RED PESTO SAUCE

Make your own sauce using the recipe from Act Two: Pesto Pasta Salad (see p.70), adding tomato purée. Italian delicatessens, and supermarkets, sell superb red pesto sauce, making preparation of this dish terribly easy if you want to take that route and CHEAT! You can use your favourite pasta, but Terry protesteth against tagliatelli or spaghetti because, delicious as they may be, they are not always conducive to romance. Pressed on this point, it emerges as an antipodean antipathy to the messiness of eating: 'Lips covered in sauce, cheeks rouged with pesto, spaghetti swooping its way into all sorts of uninvited places ...' Ah ... well, hmmm ... I have to say it sounds good to me!

175 g (6oz) of your favourite fresh pasta (fusilli, rigatoni or shells)
1 small jar of red pesto sauce
2 sun-dried tomatoes, cut into small strips
2-3 sprigs fresh oregano leaves, removed from stalks

Cook the pasta following manufacturer's instructions. Drain. Add the pesto sauce and, using a wooden spoon, blend it into the pasta. Arrange on two warmed serving plates, top with sun-dried tomato strips and sprinkle with the oregano leaves. Perking-up the dish with a little Parmesan is permissible on this occasion.

FRESH HERBED CAULIFLOWER and BROCCOLI CHEESE

The wine and herb sauce in this recipe adds a piquant touch to this wholesome dish.

1 baby cauliflower
1 equivalent-sized head of broccoli
1 cup of vegetable stock (see p.24)
30 g (2 tbsp) low-fat cheese, grated

For the sauce:

15 g (1 tbsp) corn flour
15 ml (1 tbsp) vegetable stock
15 ml (1 tbsp) semi-skimmed milk
30 ml (2 tbsp) dry white wine
5 g (1 tsp) freshly chopped parsley
5 g (1 tsp) freshly chopped mint
5 g (1 tsp) freshly chopped thyme
Ground black pepper

Trim the cauliflower and broccoli, cutting a decent cross into the base of the stems so they will cook more easily. Place both in a saucepan so that the stems sit on the bottom. Pour in the cup of vegetable stock. Bring to the boil, then simmer for about 8-10 minutes or until tender. Meanwhile, in a small bowl, mix together the corn flour with a little of the wine. When fully blended (no lumps!) add the rest of the wine, vegetable stock and milk. Put to one side. When the cauliflower and broccoli are cooked, retain the stock but carefully remove the vegetables from the saucepan and place in a small oven-proof dish. Next, put the stock saucepan over a low heat and, while stirring (important!), add the corn flour mixture; bring slowly to the boil, stirring all the time, until it thickens. Turn down the heat to simmer, then add the herbs. Finally, pour the sauce over the top, sprinkle the grated cheese over it and place under a hot grill for about 3-5 minutes until the cheese bubbles and browns.

RADDICCIO and LOLLO ROSSO LETTUCE SALAD

Definitely a 'when breaths co-mingle...' salad but quite sensational!

12 stoned black olives
Olive oil
5 g (1 tsp) fennel seeds
1 garlic clove, thinly sliced
2-3 Raddiccio lettuce leaves
2-3 Lollo Rosso lettuce leaves
Lemon juice
Ground black pepper

Place the olives in a small bowl. Coat them generously with olive oil, sprinkle lightly with fennel seeds and the sliced garlic, and leave to marinate for about an hour. When ready to serve, tear the lettuce leaves, place them into a salad bowl, sprinkle with olive oil and a little lemon juice then fold in the black olive mixture. Freshly ground black pepper provides the finishing touch.

AVOCADO with CURRIED YOGHURT and MANGO CHUTNEY

This tangy starter sharpens the taste buds and works wonderfully with warm nan bread.

150 ml (¼ pt) Greek yoghurt
5 g (1 tsp) curry powder
Drop of Tabasco sauce
1 spring onion, finely chopped
2-4 slices of cucumber, chopped finely
1 ripe avocado halved and seed removed
Mango chutney

In a bowl, mix the yoghurt, curry powder, Tabasco, spring onion and cucumber. Spoon into the avocado halves and top each with 1 tsp of mango chutney.

SMOKED SALMON SALAD in JACKET POTATOES

A new twist to an old winter favourite.

Two medium-size potatoes, washed and scrubbed
Small packet of smoked salmon, cut into small pieces
45 ml (3 tbsp) fromage frais
Juice of ½ lemon
15 g (1 tbsp) chopped chives
Ground black pepper
Red pepper, finely chopped for garnish

Place the potatoes in a high oven and cook until tender – up to 45-50 minutes, depending on size. Meanwhile, in a bowl, blend together the salmon, fromage frais, lemon juice, chives and freshly ground black pepper. When potatoes are ready, split halfway down the centre, fluff with a fork, and divide the filling between both. Sprinkle chopped pepper on top and serve.

SPINACH and CARROT MOUSSE

A deliciously colourful generous starter or main course accompaniment to enjoy with plain grilled fish, chicken or pork. This needs a little time so cook with a cocktail on the counter (see Act One).

225 g (8 oz) fresh spinach
½ tsp nutmeg
½ tsp ground ginger
1 small onion, chopped
225 g (8 oz) carrots, peeled and sliced
3 egg whites
Grated cabbage and carrot, for garnish
Oil and white wine vinegar, for dressing garnish

Wash and trim the spinach and cook for 5-6 minutes in very little water (the steam does the work). Drain (but keep the water) thoroughly and liquidise with the nutmeg and ginger and put to one side. Next, cook the onion and carrots in the spinach water for about 8-10 minutes until the carrots are soft; again, liquidise and also put to one side. Whisk the egg whites until frothy and firm and fold half into each purée. In a small greased loaf tin (or better still, a Pyrex or soufflé dish) spoon the spinach purée, and top that with the carrot purée. Stand the tin or dish in a bain marie (a roasting pan with just enough water to rise half-way up the side of the dish) and put in the oven for 1 hour, at 180C/350F/gas mark 4, or until set. When cooked, the mousse should be firm to the touch. Turn on to a serving plate with a base of fine-shredded cabbage and carrot, sprinkled with a little olive oil and white wine vinegar.

CREAMY FISH PIE

I love comfort food and this is top of my chart – comfort food to put him in the mood!

225 g (½ lb) cod - or haddock - fillets, skinned
50 g (2 oz) button mushrooms
150 ml (¼ pt) semi-skimmed milk
10 g (½ oz) low-fat spread
20 g (1 oz) whole meal flour
5 g (¼tsp) fennel seeds
350 g (12 oz) new potatoes, washed and mashed with their skins
30 ml (2 tbsp) low-fat yoghurt
Almond flakes

Place the cod and mushrooms in a saucepan, pour in the milk, bring to the boil then cover and simmer for 15-20 minutes. Remove the fish on to a plate but reserve the liquid. Flake the fish and with the mushrooms, put to one side. Melt the low-fat spread in another saucepan. When fully melted, remove from the heat momentarily while you stir in the flour. Return to a low heat and pour in the milk from the cooked fish, along with the fennel seeds. When the sauce begins to thicken, carefully add the flaked fish and mushrooms. Spoon the mixture into a 725 ml (1¼ pt) ovenproof dish and put to one side.

Creaming the potatoes comes next. This can be done in advance and makes preparation of the final dish a lot easier. Cook the potatoes and, when soft, mash them, leaving on their skins. Whisk in the yoghurt, and spoon the mixture evenly over the fish base. Sprinkle almond flakes on top and bake in the oven (220C/400F/gas mark 6) for about 30 minutes, until the potato turns golden brown and the almonds have toasted.

VALENTINE RED SALAD

A romantic blend of tempestous tomatoes, red peppers, impetuous radishes and sensual strawberries with a sun-dried tomato dressing.

2 medium Italian tomatoes, sliced thinly
1 red pepper, de-seeded and cut into thin slivers across the whole pepper
3-4 radishes, sliced thinly
5-6 strawberries, hulled and quartered lengthways
Olive oil

Red wine vinegar or balsamic vinegar
15 g (1 tbsp) sun-dried tomatoes, chopped
Salt and freshly ground black pepper
Fresh basil for garnish

Simply layer the tomatoes, pepper and radishes and place the strawberries in a cluster on top. Finally, in a jar mix together 3 parts olive oil to 1 part vinegar, add the sun-dried tomatoes, salt and pepper to taste and shake vigorously. Pour over the salad and garnish with several basil leaves.

CHICKEN BREASTS STUFFED with MANGO and CREAM CHEESE

This is a simple but tasty dish that can be prepared and on the table in minutes. If you'd like the chicken breasts to be even tastier, marinate them in dry sherry with a little chopped mint for an hour or two beforehand. Try it with the Tomato Salad and Satsuma Dressing (see p. 218).

2 skinned thick chicken breasts
1 ripe mango, peeled, de-seeded and
pulp slivered thinly
30 g (2 tbsp) low-fat cream cheese
Mint, chopped
15 ml (1 tbsp) vegetable oil
Salt and freshly ground pepper

With your hand flat on one chicken breast, use a sharp knife to cut sideways through the flesh so that the knife protrudes on the other side. Be sure to leave both ends intact. Repeat with the other breast. In a small bowl, fold together the mango slivers, cream cheese and a little chopped mint. Stuff the mixture into the chicken breasts (don't worry if it spills out slightly – you can 'garnish' with it later). In a small frying pan, heat the oil – adding a little salt and pepper to taste – and, at the same time, heat your grill to high. Put the chicken breasts into the pan and cook them for about 8-10 minutes over a medium heat without turning but basting just once. Next, cook the top of the breasts by placing the pan under a hot grill for a further 6-8 minutes until turning golden brown. Serve from the pan immediately, with any excess filling spooned over or next to the breasts. Garnish with a little mint.

BAKED TROUT with PARSNIP PURÉE and BRIE

Here's a thrilling trio of tastes – a fabulous fish, a valued veggie and a fromage of finesse. Ingredients of anticipation.

Juice of 2 limes
45-60 ml (3-4 tbsp) olive oil
15 g (1 tbsp) fresh basil, chopped
Freshly ground black pepper
2 rainbow trout, trimmed, cleaned with scales removed – allow 225-275 g (8-10 oz) per person
250 g (½ lb) parsnips, washed, peeled and cut into small slices
1 spring onion, chopped
15 g (½ oz) low-fat spread
60 g (2 oz) brie, thinly sliced
Slices of lime
White wine

First, in a small jug make a marinade of lime juice, olive oil, basil and black pepper. Score the trout three or four times on either side and lay them in the marinade for at least one hour. Next, simmer the parsnips in boiling water for about 5-6 minutes until tender. Drain, cool a little and purée in a blender along with the spring onion and low-fat spread. Transfer to a small oven-proof dish and layer the brie slices on top. Put to one side. Heat oven to 200C/400F/gas mark 6, remove the trout from the marinade and lay them in a shallow baking dish. Put a few slices of lime on the top of each fish and pour over about 2-3 tbsp white wine. Put both dishes into the oven and bake for about 20-25 minutes, basting the trout occasionally. When ready, serve the trout with the purée on the side, perhaps with boiled new potatoes and a little chopped beetroot.

HONEY-GLAZED GRILLED FRUITS

Few desserts are as nourishing or wonderful to look at as this pot pourri of your favourite fruits. Allow yourself the luxury of a little tangy sorbet on the side.

Honey
1 ripe pear, peeled and sliced
1 red apple, peeled and sliced
1 orange, peeled and cut into wedges
1 ripe banana, peeled and sliced
Cinnamon
Chopped mixed nuts

Put a small low-sided, oven-proof casserole onto the hob and add about 15 ml (1 tbsp) of honey. Gently melt it and add the fruits – side by side or mixed as preferred. Sprinkle a little cinnamon on top and let the fruit simmer over a low heat for about 5 minutes. Meanwhile, heat the grill. Remove dish from the hob, pour over a little more honey, sprinkle the nuts on top and cook under a high grill for a further 5 minutes until the honey begins to sizzle. Serve immediately.

POLYNESIAN FRUIT KEBAB

A taste of the islands to take you to paradise.

- 1 large banana
- 15 ml (1 tbsp) lime juice
- ½ papaya, peeled and cut into chunks
- 90 g (3 oz) large black grapes
- ¼ Ogen or Honeydew melon, peeled and cut into chunks
- 1 large peach, cut into chunks
- 10 g (2 tsp) low-fat spread
- 15 ml (1 tbsp) honey
- 5 g (1 tsp) sesame seeds

Cut the banana into 8 pieces and sprinkle with 1 tsp of lime juice. On to four kebab skewers, alternate pieces of all the fruits. Preheat your grill to high then, in a saucepan on a low heat, gently warm the low-fat spread, honey and remaining lime juice. Covering the base of your grill-pan with foil (to catch the juices), lay the kebabs on the rack, brush them with the heated mixture, and grill for about 2-3 minutes, turning once.

Sprinkle the kebabs with sesame seeds and grill for a final 2-3 minutes. Pour any warmed juice over the kebabs and serve with creamy low-fat yoghurt.

GREEK YOGHURT with HONEY and PASSION FRUIT

A traditional Greek breakfast dish, but with the added infusion of passion fruit, it becomes a dish to be enjoyed any night of the week too.

Greek yoghurt
Honey
Pulp of 2-3 passion fruit (include seeds!)

How you serve this is very much to your own taste. In a large loving cup, simply place two generous helpings of Greek yoghurt. Make a well with a spoon, spoon in the passion fruit and finally, trickle honey over the top and indulge yourselves. One portion with two spoons is our way!

CURTAIN CALLS

Me and Tel, my Fizz Wizz from Oz.

THUMBS UP

Over the years I have been asked to endorse many products, but I have agreed to only a few. The simple reason is that, unless I have tried and tested the product myself over a sensible time span and as a result can say with absolute conviction, 'This works for me. I believe it will work for you' I won't endorse it. Here are products which I use and am happy and enthusiastic to recommend as part of my Fizzical fitness, lifestyle and food programme.

(1) MAGIMIX

The Rolls-Royce of food processors. With blades made from French Sabatier steel, Magimix is easy to use, has a powerful motor drive and always handles everything I throw into it. With a wide and clever range of functions and accessories, it will chop, purée, blend, knead, liquidise, slice and grate in the blink of any eye. It is a wonderful time-saver, easy on the ear and a firm, favourite tool of many chefs I know and admire.

(2) GYMBODY 8 and TOPTONE 12.

You may have seen my advertisements for Slendertone products. Everywhere I go, people ask me 'Does it work?' The answer is an unqualified 'yes'. The battery-operated units send gentle pulses to your muscles by electronic muscle stimulation. It is a pleasant sensation and the important aspect is the complete portability. You wear the control unit on a waist belt linked to easy-application, stick-on pads. You can do the washing up, shopping, gardening, send the kids off to school or make your fat burner soup while you are 'working out'. A 40-minute programme is the equivalent of 240 sit-ups. It is a complement to your regular fitness programme not a substitute; and it's brilliant for those times when you don't have time to exercise. Well, now you do!

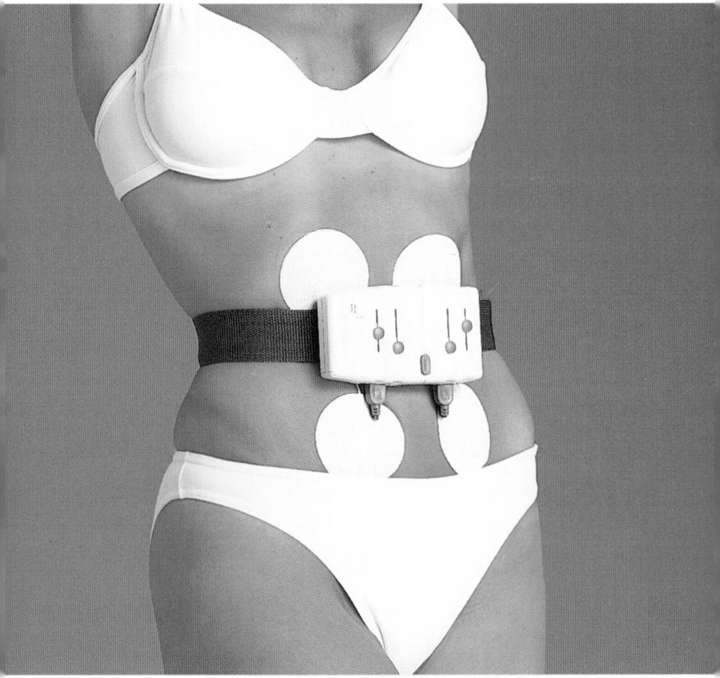

SECOND CURTAIN CALL

FEED YOUR FACE

Here's a face pack with a difference. Yoghurt and porridge oats. 'On yer bike, Harris!' I hear you cry, but this face pack is not to be sniffed at (certainly not if you get

any up your nostrils). This is a gloriously messy thing to do so perhaps the bath is the best place to try it out. It goes like this: **Half a cup of porridge oats**
1 teaspoon of honey 1 tablespoon of yoghurt
1 egg white (optional) to harden the mix

Mix to a smooth-ish paste and apply generously to the face and neck, avoiding the eyes. Leave on for 15 minutes (with egg white, 5 or 10 minutes only). Wash off with lukewarm water then splash face and neck with cold water. Feel and see the difference. It's Fizzical! Whatever is left over will stay fresh in the fridge for a couple of days and can be used up.

FINALE FIZZ-TIP

The FIZZ DE-STRESSER. Sleep is important to me. Essential, in fact. Sometimes you need to gear-down before gearing-up. In a rehearsal room or the office, when others go out for lunch into the hubbub and clang! clang! clang! of the world outside, try this: Set an alarm to ensure you are not worried about the time factor. Lie or sit with your feet and legs up on a chair. Close your eyes, soft music or cotton wool in your ears. Stop! Clear your mind. Think blank. With your eyes closed, continue 'looking' until you literally see dark green or soft black (search for it, it's there!). Now you're ready for your Fizzical Forty Winks.

On wakening, find your Fizz Food Bag, eat and drink water. When everyone else returns, you'll be ready for the 'Let's go!'FIZZICAL FORTY WINKS – DO IT!

ANITA HARRIS is one of Britain's most popular and best-loved entertainers. A multi-award-winning singer, actress and dancer, among her trophies are awards for 'Performer of the Year' and 'Concert and Theatrical Performer of the Year', many silver and gold discs for international chart successes and a double gold disc celebrating two million sales of her record-breaking hit 'Just Loving You'. Anita has starred frequently at the London Palladium, famously as 'Grizabella' in Andrew Lloyd Webber's Cats, and critical acclaim greeted her leading role portrayals in many plays, including *Bell, Book and Candle* and Ruth Rendell's *House of Stairs*. Her own long-running television series *Jumbleland* won a citation from the Canadian government for its high standards. Her BBC Television Special *The Television Machine* was a hit at the Montreux Festival and the brilliant and innovative stage show *Anita Harris – The Act* won seventeen theatre awards. She has hosted her own BBC radio and television series and is a frequent star presenter on the television shopping channel QVC. Over the years Anita has written many articles on cookery. She relaxes in Portugal, lives in London, enjoys swimming, working-out, experimenting in the kitchen and using her husband as a food taster. She is happily married to the writer, director and painter Mike Margolis.

TERRY PRITCHARD comes from the energetic world of commercial radio and television in Sydney, Australia. Beginning as an announcer with country radio stations, he joined 2SM in Sydney in 1964, where he worked in the Commercials Production Unit as a writer/producer, then to ATN Channel 7. Moving to London in 1966, Terry tasted British Record Chart success singing in two pop groups, 'Colours of Love' and 'Year One' with another fledgling singer, Elaine Paige. He was Radio and Television Publicity Officer at the Associated British Picture Corporation and MGM/EMI and was Unit Publicist for many major films, an area in which he worked for twenty years and is a respected expert. Feature writer for *Screen International* from the turn of the 1990s, his love for and knowledge of cooking and good food is inherited from his mother who ran a distinguished catering company and the famous restaurant 'The Petite Colony' on the south coast of New South Wales.

- RECIPE INDEX -